A SURVIVOR'S GUIDE
TO REVERSING
FIBROMYALGIA

A SURVIVOR'S GUIDE TO REVERSING FIBROMYALGIA

THE OWNER'S MANUAL FOR FIBROMYALGIA

ROBERT BRILL, MBA

TATE PUBLISHING
AND ENTERPRISES, LLC

Published by Tate Publishing & Enterprises, LLC
127 E. Trade Center Terrace | Mustang, Oklahoma 73064 USA
1.888.361.9473 | www.tatepublishing.com

Tate Publishing is committed to excellence in the publishing industry. The company reflects the philosophy established by the founders, based on Psalm 68:11,
"The Lord gave the word and great was the company of those who published it."

Book design copyright © 2014 by Tate Publishing, LLC. All rights reserved.
Cover designs by Lauren Nicole Brill and Anne Gatillo
Interior design by Jake Muelle

Published in the United States of America

ISBN: 978-1-62854-853-2
1. Self-Help / General
2. Health & Fitness / Diseases / General
13.11.13

ACKNOWLEDGEMENTS

When I finally had enough of the suffering that fibromyalgia (FM) can cause, I decided to write about it in hopes that it could change the lives of those suffering like me. Easier said than done, as this topic is still so far from being understood, further complicated, and misunderstood by so many medical professionals. Since the American College of Rheumatology first developed the criteria for classifying fibromyalgia as an illness in 1990, the truth about the illness has slowly been unraveled by research groups, clinicians, and pharmaceutical companies (rheumatology.org).

My family helped to drive my ambitions by remaining understanding and compassionate throughout the many difficult years. It is with great love and respect for my wife Krista and my daughter Lauren who have given me the strength to push forward every day and to strive for wellness in the face of illness. And to my parents who supported me and stayed with me through the rigorous times when almost no one else did. They understood more than anyone what it means to live with the complexities of a misunderstood, invisible illness.

It is with special consideration that I thank a few members of my wellness team that have helped me to arrive at a place where I could accept my illness and learn to cope with its many challenges. Dr. David Vallance has been my rheumatologist for the last few years and in that time he has taught me the importance of self-management as it relates to regaining an improved quality of life-despite the presence of pain and fatigue and other fibromyalgia symptoms. Dr. Vallance is a credit to physicians everywhere and provides a gift few physicians offer to individuals struggling with fibromyalgia; professionalism, kindness, and a search for the truth.

Another integral member of my wellness team is Dr. Bonnie Parker, a very gifted and compassionate clinical psychologist. Dr. Parker has been my psychologist for over 3 years and in that time she has helped me regain control of my life and go from being virtually bedridden and a victim, to learning how to find hope in hopelessness, and become a champion of my illness. Dr. Parker understands what it means for a patient to suffer significant symptoms, devastating loss, and disabling depression in the face of chronic illness.

And where would we be without inspiration? Throughout my illness, I had the pleasure of meeting Dr. Daniel Clauw, the leading fibromyalgia and chronic pain researcher out of the University of Michigan. Dr. Clauw has paved the way for patients to successfully learn to live with their chronic illnesses and has been an inspiration to me throughout my journey. Dr. Clauw has impacted many people with his oratory. I remained positive as I searched for wellness, knowing there were still heroes of medicine on the side of progress.

TABLE OF CONTENTS

FOREWORD

When you are affected by illness, whether it is you who are directly affected or a family member, your life becomes redefined. And when your illness includes chronic symptoms, it is a day-to-day testament to your strength and attitude. With chronic pain affecting everything you do every day, you struggle with the concept and reason with the idea of acceptance, and you may even ask, *why me?*

It is not uncommon to go through a type of mourning process as you adjust to your symptoms, and you may even come to a true acceptance of the reality of your illness and the pain it causes you, which is what I feel you have to do to get beyond the illness. Essentially, that is what your first goal should be—accepting your illness.

Forget what you think you know about fibromyalgia. Read this book with an open mind and a clear perspective. Once you get your head in the game, everything gets a bit easier, and once you gain a thorough understanding of the illness, it is all downhill going forward as you begin the process of *reversing fibromyalgia.*

Chronic pain is misunderstood in our society. Until you have to confront it, you may disregard its meaning or true impact. Fibromyalgia sufferers have a unique relationship with pain and its related symptoms. Most of what we complain about is coined *our opinion* and highly disregarded by physicians and society. Fibromyalgia happens to be stuck in an extended infancy stage of research, and present treatment is not very effective. A cure is just not advocated for by comparison to so many other chronic illnesses deemed *real* by the medical field.

There is no cure for many chronic illnesses today, but what makes fibromyalgia so difficult to live with is the blanket misconceptions about its validity and the lack of scientific evidence in the lab, not to mention the broad range of symptoms that have been grouped together as a syndrome and *thrown in a wastebasket*. Plus, many clinicians still argue that people with fibromyalgia are suffering from depression or are hypochondriacs.

My goal is to help advance the field of fibromyalgia and to help the world understand that fibromyalgia is a viable disease capable of disabling results if not managed properly. I have dedicated my life to the advancement of fibromyalgia. If you are reading this, I am sorry that you have joined me in the fibromyalgia battle. But if you keep reading, you will learn how to ensure that this illness does not consume you and become the fight of your life.

I hope you can find some of the answers you are seeking in these pages. I hope this book helps you understand fibromyalgia, from science to psychology, and from dealing with loss to learning how to cope. I hope you learn to gain control of your illness. I hope you find this book informative and that it analyzes what you find confusing. And finally, I hope it gives you the strength and teaches you to find hope at those times when you are hopeless. I want you to learn how to no longer be a victim and a prisoner of the illness and rejoin your life. I want you to learn to be humble at a time when that seems impossible. Accepting your illness can be the first and healthiest step toward your recovery. This will put you one more step in control of your illness and in control of your life again. You will learn how to gain control of your nutrition and exercise, your relaxation and breathing, your sleep hygiene, and your wellness team. Knowledge will move you from defeat to empowerment, and it will be the key to reversing fibromyalgia. This book closely examines fibromyalgia from early onset to minimizing your disease activity. It discusses the complexity of the illness and describes actions you can take to achieve wellness. The top elements concerning fibro are hormones, nutrition, exercise, and sleep.

ABOUT THE AUTHOR

I have had fibromyalgia for almost two decades, which is all of my adult life. I have never viewed life from a healthy perspective. I have spent much of that time researching fibromyalgia and chronic pain and studying for my PhD in health psychology so that I may advance the field of fibromyalgia. For me, fibromyalgia began as a virus that hit me hard and never really went away. Year after year, I acquired more symptoms, was diagnosed with illnesses, and the pain and fatigue seemed to gradually get worse and never completely go away. The majority of what I have written about is from my first-hand experience as an FM patient and long-time sufferer. This book is a product of eighteen years of practice learning to live with fibromyalgia.

Over the years, I went to different doctors when my symptoms would get bad enough that they were hindering some aspect of my life, and typically I got bumped around to a few different specialists until someone would eventually say, "It's time to get over it," or "It must be in your head," or "Your depression is causing your symptoms," or "Your symptoms are psychosomatic," and finally I would just give up and quit looking for answers, go home and suck it up. And since I did not have a background in medicine, it was difficult to get taken seriously. When you factor in the effect that the illness has had on me, some days I wonder how I got past the bedroom.

I was discharged as a patient from four doctors in twelve years because *they* lacked the knowledge to help me. I did not get a diagnosis of fibromyalgia until 2009 from a rheumatologist, who discharged me six months later and told me it was time I got over it because in his opinion, everyone can work through FM, and this was not a disabling illness despite that I had not have reported to him being bed ridden. Ironically, he wrote in my chart that he acknowledged all of my symptoms and validated my concerns month after month. Right at that moment, I realized that I may be in trouble. I had a rheumatologist who made a legitimate diagnosis, he validated my symptoms and treated me for six months, unsuccessfully, and then discharged me refusing to help me anymore when none of *his* treatments worked. Then he referred me to a physiatrist, who claimed to understand fibromyalgia, who prescribed me Oxycontin, Cyclobenzaprine, and Tramadol and said, "Good luck." He also prescribed physical therapy for one month, of which he said would get me *back to normal.*

In my second visit, when I questioned this treatment approach, he yelled at me for questioning his authority, discharged me as a patient, and wrote a letter to my last two doctors and to my disability provider, explaining that I was an insubordinate, depressed patient who refuses to listen to his doctor. Be careful how you talk to physicians. This was the typical cycle of poor treatment I had grown to understand as *normal* for fibromyalgia.

Since then, I have talked to many people who have had similar experiences with physicians and realized that as hard to swallow as that was, it was part of what motivated me to press on and advocate for myself. Don't let the physicians you have seen so far define your road to recovery, especially if you have had experiences like the one I described above. Your best defense is to learn as much as you can about your illness and figure out your treatment approach. *Be your own advocate.* Everyone seems to have a slightly different needs approach, even if we all share the same group of symptoms. I am working every day for a cure, but I am also working everyday on getting myself through each day, and I have to remind myself that if I ever get there, it will be because I never quit, not because I had physicians lining up to help or that I stumbled upon the cure in the form of a pill—that will be a long way down the road.

My goal is to educate you about your illness and to teach you the survival skills necessary to *not* become lost to the illness and to avoid as much of the negativity and comorbidity from happening to you along the way. When you have to deal with symptoms, especially pain that never goes away, you have to learn to accept a higher degree of pain as your new baseline. You *can* learn to readjust your pain thresholds and breaking points. You will find a new appreciation of lower levels of pain when they finally reappear.

I think when you have a chronic illness you become adept at acting day in and day out. You do not truly want your friends and family to know what is actually happening on a play by play, and you certainly do not want to continuously add to their worry and to their stress load, which is likely already maxed out, so you keep your mouth shut. I am sure you already have faced ridicule and doubt by some and often fibro patients are often demoralized by the medical community.

Pain became my motivation, and pain was interwoven into every single thing I did every day, including making decisions for today, tomorrow, and years to come. To make it through most days, planning becomes everything. From planning out your day based on your energy budget you think you have to work with today, to making purchases, creating budgets, planning for vacation, deciding where you are going to live, or the car you are going to drive.

But pain is as good of a motivational force as any, in fact some days pain will allow you to super achieve versus other days when you feel defeated. Don't deny the fact that some days the pain will cripple you physically and/or emotionally. Chronic pain can quite often be the straw that broke the camel's back, so you have to be creative in your pursuit for wellness. You cannot give up. Even though you will be defeated more often than you would like, you can slowly gain ground if you remain strong-willed and with a humble attitude.

Fibromyalgia can also cause a financial burden if you are too sick to work. The snowball effect can happen fast and be devastating and it can be extremely difficult to manage a household and a family budget when all you can focus on is getting out of bed. Most of us do not have a money tree in the back yard, and few of us have enough money in the bank to get us through what can amount to years of struggles, medical bills, and disability. Eliminating your debt through lifestyle changes is a good place to start, and if you are counting on winning a Social Security disability case, you are on an eighteen-month minimum road. Fibromyalgia has only recently been recognized by the Social Security Administration as a viable illness, capable of disabling results. However, FM is still not on *the list* of guaranteed awards for Social Security, but it can be done. You may still go through a financial hardship and a rigid downsizing.

Everyone knows what it means to hurt. For most people, pain is something that exists on a check-off list. When you get injured or sick, there is almost always an end in sight, and that assumption is based on hope. You hope this pain ends soon. You hope that you feel better soon—because the alternative is unthinkable. For me the pain came one day and never left. Fatigue accompanied the pain shortly after. I would adjust my expectations of my symptoms daily and hope for the best. Pain can be on your mind twenty-four hours a day, and you have to learn how to get it off your mind.

Gaining freedom from illness was my goal and it's all about the attitude. The best treatment program that exists today coupled with lifestyle changes, proper nutrition, exercise, and so on, will only deliver you to a degree of freedom from illness. Until there are significant discoveries made in the world of FM, you may always have some degree of illness. That is a tough pill to swallow in itself, but as I said, it is all about the attitude, and it could always be worse. Once you make the necessary changes in your life, you are guaranteed to see some relief and the better you stick to a wellness regime, the better your degree of symptom relief.

Fibromyalgia research realistically needs to grow in regards to causes, diagnosis, treatments, and studies of medications, genetics, and perpetuating factors. Working on this book forced me to get up, it motivated me to get out of bed, and it was something I thought the world desperately needed. I encourage everyone with a chronic illness to educate themselves and to write as often as possible for a number of reasons—most of all it cleanses the soul.

Consider that someone can write anything they want to. What I have written about is not designed to sway you one way or another, or to sell supplements, or car magnets. What I am suggesting is that this illness is very complicated, and it is easy to forget that the information is out there, and the more you have, the better-off you are, and that hope is sometimes the only medicine that you have that works in the moment.

A lot of what I have written about in these pages I have tried, much of which did not work for me nor had any effect. What I am suggesting here is a broad range of trials that should not be tried without working with a clinician or with consent of a physician knowledgeable in FM treatment, especially mega-dosing supplements since they are medicines. So tread carefully, but keep treading.

HEALED WITHOUT BEING CURED

Recently I explained to a friend how I felt that those with chronic illnesses can be *healed without being cured*. I talk to individuals with different disabilities every day, and at times we all ask the questions, *When will the pain go away? Will I always feel this sick? What can I do to get better?*

Today, we have to accept that there is no cure for the diseases many of us have. That too is a hard pill to swallow. There is a broad gamut of treatment options available for most of us though, sometimes it just takes work to find what works with lifestyle changes to maintain your health.

So what do we do in the meantime? What do we do with the time we have to live that is after we accept our illness but before we experience symptom relief? How do we become healed without becoming cured? Hearing "you will have to go home and learn to live with this for the rest of your life" is not a realistic answer for anyone, even chronically ill patients.

Almost nothing really fixes the problem in fibro but numerous things treat the symptoms. And for a large population of chronically ill individuals in the United States alone, medicine has failed to provide them any benefits or relief. Without going into great detail, this has a compounding effect on the economy, society's medical costs, and missed time from work, and of course on the government for those who must resort to collecting disability benefits from the Social Security Disability Department.

I have had people who I have helped cope with their illness explain to me that if they do not find relief soon that they will strongly consider suicide. I ask, "What has it taken for you to arrive at that point in your life, where you are ready to end your life due to pain?" But when I think long and hard about it, which I have, it makes some sense. After all, some days I was just hanging on by a thread, and I pray that just one more disaster does not happen to me that causes me to take just one more step backwards, to gain just one more symptom, to face one more emotional loss. Suicide thoughts translate into our inner self wanting to escape from what seems like an impossible situation. How do we heal ourselves without being cured?

It cannot be as simple as accepting your illness and moving on from there, can it? I have accepted my illness—there it is. I've accepted what has happened to me. Is that a form of healing? It is my understanding that it is. It is one issue I do not have to address again. I have moved beyond that issue and I am ready for my next battle. I have also learned to laugh at my situation. I laugh as often as possible. I create cartoons to share on Facebook, I spread comedy where possible, and when I do, I know I am receiving therapeutic effects, such as endorphins being released, making me feel just a bit better. Reversing fibromyalgia is a process that begins with acceptance.

These things make up my foundation some days. They are not big commitments, they are not challenging to pursue, and they lift my spirits and those around me up a little. So that being said, I have found healing in the shape of acceptance. It is like a cure nonetheless. No one can take that from me and I like being the one who can provide this for anyone reading this or for anyone needing something, or for anyone missing something, but not sure what it is.

Every day I have my foundation to stand on, and from there I begin to develop principles with which to live by, to find happiness with, and to help others with. I also write a blog about many things that are real for many people. When you are ill, you are often left with too much down time and sick or not, it is still your down time and your choice of what to do with that time. After you meet the basic needs in your life, it is time to find the next thing; the next chapter in your life that will become your next cure. You are very unlikely to find it in your doctor's office or at your pharmacy. You have to search your life and passions and find that thing that gives new meaning to your illness—and *you* have to do that.

Time is going to pass whether you are ready for it or not, whether you are excited for it or not, and whether you are sick or not. You get to make the choice to be sick and have a rotten life, or you can choose to be sick and to accept your illness as is and begin to move on with plans for the future. Some people live life in a wheelchair, some without sight; you get to live life with a chronic illness. You can choose to be healed without being cured. It is your responsibility to live your life to the fullest, sick or not. You need to find a way. I did it. I was not lucky, and I was not symptom free. I did it with every constraint in the world thrown in my face. I expect no less from you. If you do not know how and want straight answers-then continue reading and you may find something that will benefit your search for wellness. Your pain will teach you a valuable lesson if you let it and if you are dissatisfied with your life, making changes will lead to growth.

To be healed without being cured requires taking actions, changing behaviors, eliminating catastrophic thinking, and increasing positive reinforcement. It requires eating right, exercising, cognitive behavioral therapy, pacing, and a strong attitude. Educating yourself gives you a broader perspective of your illness as well as what is involved in achieving wellness.

Psychology shapes the biology. Fibromyalgia is a biological illness that like most other illnesses has the ability to make changes in the brain which impact the psychology leading to numerous emotional and psychological issues, making you more ill. It is when you get control of your life and all of the aspects I discuss in this book that reverses your illness. By making these changes you are going to make positive, physical changes in your brain that will direct you toward wellness.

Illness paradigms are our predisposed beliefs and feelings about our illness that stand in the way of wellness—like catastrophizing. The paradigm shift occurs when you stop being the victim and suddenly see things not just correctly, but optimistically. This is the beginning of the path to wellness. Change the way you view your illness and you change your illness outcome.

FIBROMYALGIA 101

Today, fibromyalgia is classified as a syndrome, not a disease. FM is fairly common and grouped into the category of central pain syndromes. FM is a controversial diagnosis partly due to the lack of a concensus in the medical field as to the specifics of the illness. The main characteristics of fibromyalgia are widespread pain, tenderness, and fatigue. Theoretically, when you have FM, you likely have bacterial infections, hormone dysfunctions, metabolic imbalances, viruses, fungal issues, neurologic issues, digestive issues, cardiac issues, a genetic predisposition, etc. Research suggests that FM may have some developmental factors like genetics, autoimmune dysfunction, nutritional deficiencies, environmental factors, or connective tissue disease, among other things. Likely it's 50 percent genetics and 50 percent environmental.

The word *fibromyalgia* comes from the Latin term for fibrous tissue *fibro* and the Greek term for muscle *myo* and pain *algia* (nih.gov). I am not a big fan of the name or the definition of fibromyalgia, because I feel it does not accurately describe what is actually happening and that adds to the poor reputation of the illness that we know too well.

For decades, FM has been viewed by the medical field in unprofessional terms. It has changed names several times as new developments are made, such as hysterical paroxysm, muscular rheumatism (1600s), myalgia, and fibrositis (1904) and my favorite, tender lady syndrome (arthritis.gov). The term fibromyalgia was coined in 1976 by Dr. Hugh Smythe, (Clauw, Fitzcharles, Goldberg, Katz, Mease, Wolfe, Yunus in 2010), but it has wreaked havoc since Biblical times. FM was thought to be a muscular disease until no link to muscles could be found. Then it was considered an autoimmune disease but with nothing proving wrong with the immune system. The most current, widely accepted cause is a malfunction of the central nervous system, even though tests will confirm otherwise. And that really does not appear to be causal at this point.

FM is often considered a condition in the arthritis family but is not a disease of the joint, and typically there is no inflammation involved. This is the main reason the name was changed from fibrositis to fibromyalgia in 1976. And since no permanent damage is said to occur in the nerves, muscles, or joints, FM is not considered degenerative even though many of us feel like we got worse for years, often deconditioning occurs versus degeneration. I anticipate the name fibromyalgia will change again in the future to more accurately describe it.

I support the theory that genetics plays a significant role in whether you develop FM or not, followed by lifestyle or an environmental trigger. If you consider the ratio of men to women who have fibro, it is a one-to-nine ratio. This suggests a genetic link, however, since women in general are more *tender* and sensitive to pain than men, I imagine this number would be less for women. I think it is logical at this point to deduce that you may be predisposed, as in many other diseases, and at some point in your life, something triggers the illness like an infection, trauma, childbirth, or another disease, etc.

Fibromyalgia can cause significant pain and fatigue, and it can interfere with a person's ability to carry on normal activities. I personally have not met many people at all in my eighteen years with the illness whose major complaint is tender points. And sadly, all we had until recently to diagnose FM was eleven of eighteen tender points presenting at one time and pain in all four quadrants for three months (rheumatology.org). I find tender points to be a useless indicator for fibromyalgia.

When this illness was transitioning from being believed to be a muscular disease to *something else*, all they had as a common *physical* symptom that would be acceptable to the American College of Rheumatology (ACR), the Centers for Disease Control and Prevention (CDC), and the general field of medicine was the tender points, and this criterion was originally established for research only.

Since then, there are so many other symptoms in common that could be used for diagnosis, but most have yet to be considered to meet the criteria. I have had many physicians agree with my original diagnosis from a rheumatologist that I do in fact have FM, even though the areas on my body that are tender change from day to day, and I do not think I have ever had more than nine, I had eight tender points on the day of my diagnosis. This may also contribute to the doubt by some physicians that this illness is real. It is not uncommon for tender points to come and go like many other symptoms.

A patient medical history is necessary to make a diagnosis that is acceptable by most organizations, because traditionally your doctor was looking for a history of mental illness to assign cause for the disease, which still happens often today. Since fibromyalgia is a central pain syndrome, diagnosis can in reality be made in about five minutes, assuming all other diseases have been ruled out, just by talking to the patient.

Central sensitization is a popular theory, which suggests that FM sufferers have a low threshold for pain due to an increase in sensitivity in the brain to signals in pain.; i.e. volume turned up. It has been recently established using brain imaging that there is a dysfunction of the central nervous system (CNS) responsible for the high levels of pain sensitivity seen in FM. It is suggested that the problem is a combination between the CNS and the brain.

In theory, any incident that results in injury from an accident or at the biological level can cause hypersensitivity to that affected area. This leads to central sensitization and is apparent as your CNS reacts to chronic pain. This seems like a logical research direction to go but so did so many other directions prior to this theory.

Pain can be amplified for a few reasons, and the first is the thought that more nerve connections develop in your spine that can result from chemical changes. Research shows that the brain can adapt to environmental changes known as *neural plasticity* (stanford.edu). We can also induce positive brain plasticity. Research also shows that the stress that overwhelms your ability to manage that stress negatively affects brain development. This stress can be cumulative. So stress alters and remodels the developing brain, leading to illness. So we leverage neural plasticity to promote wellness. In short, the brain is malleable and subject to changes from our genetic predisposition and our environment. Additionally, neurotransmitters that transmit pain also can increase causing a rise in chronic pain stimuli. There is said to be a delayed, exaggerated, and inappropriate autonomic nervous system (ANS) response to typical stimuli in FM. There is a chemical known as argenine vasopressin that is responsible for preventing the fight-or-flight response to stress. With FM, your body does not recognize the appropriate reaction to this function and it does not shut off. Your body tricks your mind into believing you are in constant jeopardy of injury, while your pain centers are going wild. This is still somewhat of a mystery to medical researchers today.

The definition and classification of FM has changed since its discovery, and science has been able to eliminate previously stated facts or theories about the illness. The diagnosis is considered specific and unique but is actually vague and suggested that it is easy to fake. Further, its reputation is what keeps this illness from gaining the appropriate research dollars necessary to make advancements in the field, as well as gain the overdue respect in the medical field, and finally the much needed support from the Social Security Administration.

I think ignorance is to blame for the reputation that FM has specifically as it relates to severity and the tiny percentage of individuals who exaggerate or malinger for attention. It is difficult to determine if someone truly is disabled by this illness by reason of definition or opinion because depending on which physician you see, will be the hinging statistic that labels who has it, how many have it, how severe it is, and considering that FM symptoms can wax and wane, for how long do they have it. The physicians have to trust their patients to some degree, but they need to have an expertise in fibro for starters.

I believe many will have FM for life to some degree. Today, many already have had it for thirty years or more. Since treatment is complicated and intermittent in the traditional form, many individuals find no relief for years. It can be a difficult time between onset of symptoms, and diagnosis, and further acceptance as a whole. This is why physicians need to be critical in accurately diagnosing and treating the illness, and further reporting the figures to the CDC. This statement is clearly defined in the broad range of statistics reporting how many people in the United States have FM. You can find logical supporting medical data that suggests anywhere from four million to twenty-five million afflicted depending on the source and if classification and diagnosis were simplified, that number would be more consistent and much higher. Especially when you consider that it can take many years to get a diagnosis. Imagine how many individuals today have fibromyalgia but are but lacking a diagnosis? My theory is that the number is closer to thirty five to forty five million worldwide. What the medical community thinks about fibromyalgia does not matter as much as what you think about it, because you are the deciding factor in if you get better or not—no one else.

Research over the last thirty five years suggests that there is a malfunction with the central nervous system with fibro. These studies show significant correlation between symptoms but weak causative relationship. The combination of pain and sleep issues is a vicious cycle on its own for FM. The pain makes sleep difficult to achieve and sleep deprivation exacerbates pain.

Additionally, I would not be thorough if I did not include chronic fatigue syndrome (CFS), in with FM, which is the case for many in the medical field. Both illnesses share characteristics and overlap in many symptoms and are even considered synonymous by many in the medical field. There are, however, defining characteristics that distinguish the two illnesses, and as such, should be treated separately, especially when consideration is placed on research dollars. I believe CFS is a symptom of FM, and not the other way around. They are different.

THE HYPOTHALAMUS

It seems one possibility is that the major malfunction in FM is that the hypothalamus stops working correctly and this leads to many other body systems working incorrectly. The hypothalamus controls the stress response by releasing corticotropin-releasing hormone activating the norepinephrine system. The basic things we do on a daily basis force this system to exacerbate our symptoms—too much, too often. Subsequently, it seems like rest and sleep no longer do their job and the viscous cycle may begin. This can cause cognition issues, hormonal issues, immune system issues, metabolic issues, infections, sleep issues, ANS issues, and many other FM symptoms.

The perpetuating cycles can be overwhelming. The hormonal issues alone can cause nearly all of one's hormones to be out of whack, the most common being the thyroid, which can slow the metabolism and contributes to the typical weight gain seen in FM patients, 35 lbs. on average. Here, one may see other issues like frequent urination, cold and heat intolerances, cognition issues, fatigue, etc., as problems. Hypothyroidism causes low-basal body temperature which leaves you susceptible to more infections.

The hypothalamus also controls the ANS, which is often seen to have multiple problems as well in FM. This is a difficult issue to target because testing is almost impossible, as are most FM issues. The ANS controls automatic functions like blood pressure, sweating, respiration, circulation, salivation, urination, digestion, hormone production and more—all problems with FM. You can quickly see how getting your symptoms under control all together and not individually can help you at least in theory. But the cycles of FM are so misunderstood today; it is hard to know what is affecting what, and what issues need to be addressed first. Treating the caboose is not helpful.

The hypothalamus sends hormones to the pituitary, which controls the thyroid, adrenal glands, ovaries, and testes and really monitors the hormone levels of all of these. Not to mention, the hypothalamus regulates numerous other hormones like human growth hormone (HGH), prolactin, and oxytocin, and since the hypothalamus directs each gland to manufacture their respective hormones, it is really responsible for the regulation of many other hormones as well. So the perpetuating part of this process is that the hypothalamus has a cause-and-effect relationship with many other body systems, as do many other body systems with each other—and they all can suppress each other. So while you may be treating your thyroid effectively, it may not be enough in the big picture, if you are not addressing the ten other issues that are being affected by something else in your body. So it is important to address everything all together. You cannot just treat one, or two, or three of your symptoms and expect to see major results. This is a major misconception in FM; one that many physicians still do not fully realize. This is why you need to find a physician who understands fibromyalgia and knows how to approach it. Beyond that, you need to manage your condition to the best of your ability.

So all these problems and you will likely test normally! I think this is one of the major reasons FM is so difficult for medical professionals to understand. History has shown that when something is wrong, evidence will show it, and in the case of FM, the evidence just is not there! The important thing to keep in mind here is that you can control a large portion of this puzzle, and you need to control what you can or you will feel worse. Figuring out what is most wrong with your body is a great place to start, and treating those issues first, and treating those issues aggressively makes most sense today. I am a big picture type of person, and I do not think most are seeing the big picture when it comes to FM as it stands, so equip yourself with as much knowledge as you can and you will be surprised how much better off you will feel.

WHAT CAUSES FIBROMYALGIA?

Fibromyalgia seems to still be a puzzle to most everyone. The cause is still unknown and may take a long time until it will be known. A number of theories exist and the popular ones are genetics, an accident, trauma, stress related, repetitive injuries, a virus or bacteria, or it may be a spontaneous illness—possibly a link between how the brain and the spinal cord process pain. FM can be a primary condition with no known cause and it can be a secondary condition with a more likely root cause like another disease, trauma, an injury, or event that may have stimulated the illness. It is possible a person's genes could suggest how painful stimuli are processed differently. There have been several genes identified that occur more frequently in FM sufferers. I have touched briefly on some of the theories and science in the pages that follow.

KNOWING IS HALF THE BATTLE: REVERSING FIBROMYALGIA

The primary focus of fibro is chronic pain and chronic fatigue. My research into fibro led me down the path of neuroscience which I think best assembles the puzzle. My findings suggest that there are a few fundamental building blocks to wellness that can be applied to fibro. I propose that the simple act of educating yourself about your illness will provide more symptom relief than any other treatment modality that exists today. Once you can get your arms around any problem, the problem begins to seem a whole lot smaller and more manageable, and suddenly solutions begin to present themselves—all through the process of understanding, and lifestyle management.

When we receive the label of fibromyalgia we begin to adjust our whole world according to that label. After we get a diagnosis, our illness finally has a label, but the questions do not end there and solutions do not begin to present themselves. Our job as a chronic pain patient just got a bit more complicated. It now becomes our job to educate ourselves and look for ways to reduce our pain, and manage our symptoms to keep us in the game and to help us avoid disability.

This concept of knowledge and understanding is universal, but western medicine does not prescribe this kind of treatment for pain relief because it puts too much effort on the patient, and it only tells part of the story. After all, patients get sick, they go to doctors for help, and they let the medicine do the work. This process works for about half the illnesses out there today, and fibro really is not one of them.

For the rest of us, we have to learn to manage our condition, and we will be the ones charged with reducing our symptoms through our efforts. The first thing we do is we change our attitude. This is where it begins. The way we feel about our illness predisposes us to the way we will react to our illness—and this translates into symptoms. If we feel hopeless, like a failure, or a reject, or angry, or cheated, etc., this toxic pessimism will become a product of our attitudes and we will feel all of these things in the form of symptoms, and physical changes in the brain occur. So these negative attributes exacerbate our current symptoms, making them go from simply present, tolerable, and manageable, to complex, extreme, and unmanageable.

Why do we have so many symptoms? The complex syndrome that is fibro is the result of many malfunctions occurring in your body at the same time. The cause seems to be all over the map, but with one common denominator—environmental trigger. I think fibro or this central pain syndrome is the cause of most or all of our *unrelated* maladies. At some point you *got* fibro. You were not born with symptoms, even though you were likely genetically predisposed. At some point in your life your body began responding to mixed signals and malfunction, causing some of your systems to also malfunction, driving your pain tolerance down which keeps you operating within a very small range between idle pain and extreme pain. This pain tolerance I am talking about is hypersensitivity with post-exertional malaise, but do we really know why this happens? The most popular theory is that this hypersensitivity of nerves from the malfunction of numerous systems causes your nerve baseline to be higher. This means you are at the cusp of pain all the time, or that your condition simply turns your pain volume up.

Is the nervous system involved? Your nervous system seems to take the brunt of the effects of all the malfunctioning, and its response is to raise your nerve sensitivity to high which is where it stays all the time. This immediately causes you to be hypersensitive to everything, and you are in pain all the time. This pain hypersensitivity is known as hyperalgesia, which is an increased response to pain, and allodynia, which is a painful response to non-painful things. The nervous system overreacts and begins a high defense strategy, resulting in a multi-symptom syndrome. So here, being sensitive to sound, light, odors, touch, or having bladder issues for example, are simple products of this malfunction.

Why do some people get fibro worse than others? Have you ever noticed that some people have mild fibro and lead normal lives with slight discomfort, while others are bedridden and the rest of us fall somewhere in between? Fibro happens to be one of those conditions that seem to be a result of *your* experiences prior to and during disease. Meaning, how you lived your life prior to fibro has a lot to do with how you react to fibro once you have it, and how well you manage your illness after diagnosis translates into your degree of symptom severity.

As a rule, those who have physically and emotionally conditioned themselves to a high degree remain healthier throughout life with less sickness, disease, and cancers. The opposite end of the spectrum is people who likely start off with a predisposition for illness, and their lifestyle *manifests into fibro*. This means how you live your life combined with environmental factors leads to fibro and fibro severity. This is tough to swallow, I know, but it makes sense once you have educated yourself on fibro, the immune system, the nervous system, genetics, and environmental factors, etc. Again, it is complex and difficult.

What is the brains role in fibro? Pain really is all in your head. That is where all pain and pain signals originate and based on your experiences, determines how you react to the pain. For example, a boxer can take a punch better than the general population. Why? Because he has conditioned himself to *understand* the pain, *accept* the pain, and *cope* with the pain to a very high degree.

Anyone can do this if they decide to do it. The brain has been trained to recognize certain pains, and to disregard overreacting to many commonly recognized pains. This boxer is less likely to experience pain much differently than this throughout his life; his brain will always accept pain differently than other people.

How does this translate to fibro? The experiences you have had in your life that you have trained your brain to accept, *or to* overreact to, determine to what degree you will later experience pain from injury or illness. This is not to suggest that a boxer will not develop a chronic pain condition at some point, but if they do, then their brains are already accepting many types and levels of pain without launching an all-out attack, or overreaction that results in hypersensitivity. It is likely that most of us are not in the same category of pain tolerance as a boxer or professional athlete, which means when fibro hit us, we were not already conditioned for high levels of pain; we had not trained our brains to understand and recognize significant pain, and thus we wind up experiencing high levels of pain with fibro.

When the brain senses it must respond to a pain stimulus, or in the case of fibro where pain is constant, the brain essentially occupies much more real estate than would normally be required to respond to a painful stimulus. Essentially in fibro, the brain operates in a more full capacity, and this translates into other body systems malfunctioning and being inhibited, and multiple symptoms begin, like, fatigue, headaches, bowel and bladder issues, infections, and post-exertional malaise, etc.

Fibro medications like Lyrica, Cymbalta, Savella, and Neurontin, etc., are geared toward promoting *calm* in the nervous system. The more you focus on your symptoms with a negative connotation, the more they are exacerbated. Our focus needs to be on controlling our nervous system. This starts and ends with understanding our condition and changing the way we think, feel, and react to it. Your physician will not tell you this.

Why do we have so much pain with fibro? It is thought that our nerve sensors become disrupted. We know that when we have an injury, our brains interpret the stimulus and reacts to it by producing a pain response—essentially to tell us something is wrong but also to tell us to do something about it—like get help. So again, your brain produces the pain according to your body's needs and to the magnitude of the injury. Minor injury is equal to minor pain response. Major injury is equal to major pain response.

Your nerve sensors tell your brain to produce pain, and how much pain to produce. Your brain produces a pain magnitude appropriate to your nerve sensors. With a chronic illness like fibro, your brain gets signals from your nerve sensors just like with an injury, *but* with fibro, your nerve sensors are on high because your nerve threshold is right at the upper limit. This is why you have more pain but also why you have constant pain with fibro. Fibro also results in more stress. When you increase your stress level, you actually *increase* the amount of nerve sensors that exist all over the body, which increases your pain experience. Your physician will not tell you this either. It is believed that *this* is the primary mechanism behind fibro. Knowledge promotes understanding and understanding translates into a reduction of nerve sensors-thereby reducing pain.

Fibro and your lifestyle. It slowly becomes apparent how leading a lifestyle congruent with poor health contributes to the proper setting for disease. Physicians suggest proper diet and exercise as a foundation for proper health as a blanket statement, and it truly does apply to fibro as well. Diet with exercise is an 80/20 phenomenon, respectively. But everything matters.

If you always eat a healthy diet of raw foods, whole foods, unprocessed foods, low fat, low carb, low sodium, and avoid the standard American diet of fast food, junk food, soda, and sweets, you are likely to live a longer, healthier life, free of disease. This is a fact proven again and again in longevity studies. I know bad things happen to good people, but again, this is *as a rule*, a rule that applies to everyone on the planet with or without disease, including us with fibro. So getting your diet as right as it can be will aid you in reversing your fibro.

If you remain active and physical, then you will likely live a longer, healthier life, free of disease, *as a rule*. Those of us, who sat around a lot, did not play sports as children and teens, watched a lot of TV, and continued to not exercise and gain weight year after year, are setting the scene for disaster. Those of us who were super overachievers, burning the candle at both ends for way too long are doing virtually the same thing—setting the scene for breakdown. We have allowed our brains to accept a lower threshold of pain, strain, and stress, and some of us have overtaxed our systems to infinity. We have allowed our muscles, joints, tendons, and ligaments to function at a reduced capacity, contrary to the way our bodies were designed to operate.

It comes down to changing the way we view pain. Pain is an emotional experience. Think positive and feel good, think negative and feel bad. It is almost that simple. Pain that becomes chronic is its own disease affecting how you interact with all stimuli, elevating all your pain responses. Everything bad in your life—stressful work environment, bad relationship, poor lifestyle, poor diet, laziness, etc.,—compounds your fibro symptoms. When you consider all of the attributes that are suspected to impact fibro like fear, the unknown, societal beliefs, family and friends accepting you with fibro, work difficulty and stress, the stress of losing your job, marriage complications associated with illness, dealing with physicians, dealing with disability providers or Social Security, financial difficulties, and then factor in all of your pain and other symptoms—you begin to see how your stress load is way more than anyone can or should have to deal with. Unknown and undealt with issues exacerbate symptoms. This stress-load maxes out our ability to live normally.

The very process of changing the way you view pain reduces the negative affect on the body. Your systems will be allowed to relax and not require so much of your brains attention, and this will lower your nerve threshold. This does two things for starters—first, since your nerve threshold is lowered, you are no longer operating in the fight-or-flight mode constantly, where the slightest stressor or activity causes a flare and puts you down for a few days with overwhelming pain and fatigue. Second, when all of these systems are allowed to relax, surprisingly, your pain level will reduce to a lower baseline-essentially taking your pain down a few notches. Will this practice make you pain free? No, it will not, but a cure is not what we are after with this approach—managing the illness and re-entering our lives is the goal here. We are reversing our illness not curing it!

WILL FIBROMYALGIA IMPROVE WITH TIME?

Since FM is classified as a chronic condition, it typically will last many years and in many cases, an entire lifetime, to varying degrees. FM is said to not be degenerative or fatal, and with no damage occurring to organs or body systems the outlook is said to be manageable. But understand this, chronic pain is a progressive disease. For many people, improvements are made to a great degree, for some, disability is inevitable. I say that because some people are not willing to manage their own lives when they are healthy much less when they become ill, and you have to manage your whole lifestyle when you have FM. If you do not do what you need to do—*what is essential to feel better*, you will surely feel worse.

Since the cause of FM is still unknown and there is no medical consensus on treatment, measurement, and longevity, significant improvement may still take a while. Remember, there is no singular confirming diagnostic test or proven effective treatment of FM. Do not misinterpret the fact that many people have been successfully treated with FM and many more never become severely ill or disabled by the disease. Only a small percentage, 8–15 percent do not fully respond to treatment. That is to say that this 8–15 percent have to work harder to find the right combination of what exactly works for them, and it may not be what the FDA has approved lately. It may be a complex lifestyle regimen that is difficult to follow but the alternative is-you remain ill.

Research is strong today versus even ten years ago, and not just in the United States. Research is really all over the map when it comes to interventions, tools, directions, and outcomes, which I think is a better way to cover more bases at once. Right now, the first goal is to control or reduce symptoms. Dream big, hope bigger!

I am very optimistic about the research being done on FM today. When I suggest that FM is a mystery or that it is misunderstood by most physicians, I am speaking about those in the general public that have not gotten *on board* yet. The great news for us is that there are new physicians getting on board every day, and there are fantastic researchers like Dr. Daniel Clauw making amazing advances in research every day. FM is not a total mystery to everyone. When you find a physician who shows a vague understanding of the illness, feel free to fire your physician and find another one.

DECONDITIONING: THE ROAD TO ILLNESS

Fibromyalgia is not degenerative but is progressive, and the less you move, the more you become deconditioned. If you don't use it, you will lose it! It is unnatural to be inactive, and when you develop fibro, your life changes in many ways. You face loss of ability, pain, fatigue, and myriad other symptoms that make life more difficult for you. This begins a cycle of *doing less*, and leads to becoming deconditioned, and causes numerous physiologic adaptations to the body.

If you think rest and inactivity are what you need with fibro, consider this—Deconditioning leads to a reduced or limited physical capacity. Our musculoskeletal system suffers the worst. It can lead to injured joints, ligaments, tendons, etc., and osteoporosis can develop. Cartilage degeneration begins, soft tissues become mature tissues, a decrease in muscle strength and endurance occurs, and weakening of the core develops. Your pain threshold can be reduced, increasing your pain, since inactivity is not what our body expects from us; it is unnatural. Physiological changes can occur in nearly every body system. Deconditioning is a slippery slope.

The less you do, the more your body will pay for it. In six weeks' time, your muscles can become 50 percent weaker. Muscles and connective tissue can become shortened and loss of bone density occurs after a few weeks of immobility. After 12 weeks, your bone density can be reduced by 50 percent. Your resting heart rate increases, your blood volume decreases, and postural orthostatic tachycardia syndrome (POTS) can develop. Clotting can increase, leading to strokes, etc. Unnatural-fluid shifts begin to occur. Pneumonia can develop, oxygen can decrease, and the heart can atrophy. You can become glucose intolerant, leading to type two diabetes. Many hormones can malfunction. You can experience constipation, malfunction of absorption, and urinary-tract infections. Body fat can increase. Anxiety and depression can set in. Your sleep-wake cycle can become disrupted. This is only a partial list of what can happen the more you become deconditioned from inactivity.

STATISTICS AND HISTORY
OF FIBROMYALGIA

It is hard to even put an estimate on the US numbers of FM. The CDC suggests the numbers are around five million (cdc. gov). The NIH claims the number is five million (nih.gov). The American Pain Foundation states that up to six million may have FM (painfoundation.org). The National Fibromyalgia Research Association concludes that there are more than six million cases in the US (nfra.net). The National Fibromyalgia Association asserts the number is closer to ten million FM patients in the US in 2010 (fmaware.org). That range may be a gross understatement since diagnosis is so difficult for so many physicians. Plus, an unknown range of five to ten million is the range differentiation of all the *official experts*. Since no one is said to die from this illness you will have any changing number of symptoms throughout your life. As I stated earlier, I feel that the number of those with FM is closer to fifteen million in the United States and another twenty million outside the United States. The prevalence of fibro is kind of a grey area. I have personally met a large number of people who fit the diagnostic criteria for fibro but do not have a diagnosis for a number of possible reasons, suggesting that the overall prevalence of fibro is much higher than reported by the CDC or the NIH. It should not take more than one visit to diagnose fibro and you should be well on your way to making changes in the first month of diagnosis. It is a travesty that all too often, fibro takes many years to diagnose, leaving the patient needlessly suffering.

I should not say no one dies from FM but rather directly from the illness as it is classified medically. There are mortality rates on the CDC Website that classifies fibromyalgia within the group of rheumatic conditions, of which does carry less than .5 percent mortality rate (cdc.gov). Depending upon your perpetuating factors or comorbid diseases which make your illness worse when not being identified or addressed by your doctor, your body may assume collateral damage in other organs or body systems. If you are one of the many patients who has little regard for managing their own care to a high degree and symptoms grow based on perpetuating factors, your body systems may begin to fail. Welcome to a minority class of people. A minority class whose numbers are greater than multiple sclerosis, lung cancer, and AIDS combined; a class of self-healing practitioners who accept the aid and support from those in the medical field who are on board with *our personal mission,* our goals, our objectives, and who align their beliefs with our vision of health.

FM is the second most common illness seen by rheumatologists, which is likely why you need a rheumatologist in your corner going through the disability process, and hopefully advocating for you. Your most respected diagnosis will come from a rheumatologist. FM typically strikes between the age of twenty and fifty-five, and is nine times more likely to affect women than men; again this 9:1 ratio is likely inflated. A hereditary link has not been 100 percent established but there are numerous individuals with family members also affected, and often, mother-child relationships are found, to me, creating a strong genetic connection (rheumatology. org). The heritable connection in first degree relatives is eight percent—significantly higher than many other illnesses. This means if your mother has fibro, you are eight times more likely to develop it at some point.

Many in the medical profession feel that FM is psychological in origin, but I think are wrong. In fact, research has proven that you are no more likely to develop depression as a result of FM, as compared to any other chronic illness (rheumatology.org).

It is interesting that many agencies in the medical field, with the exception of the NIH and the CDC, the two main researching government agencies, cannot find anything significant wrong with FM patients, but the American Association of Blood Banks (AABB) recommends those diagnosed with FM and CFS do not donate blood. While some argue that there is not a genetic variable in FM, again statistical research has shown that you are eight times more likely to get FM if there is a family history (aabb.org).

THE EVOLUTION OF FIBROMYALGIA

Details of FM as a syndrome date back to before 1500 BC but did not really begin being discovered in medical journals until the 1800s. In 1824, Dr. Balfour was the first to describe tender points. At this point FM was still considered muscular rheumatism or neurasthenia (rheumatology.org). In 1904 Sir William Gowers made the recommendation to change the name to fibrositis, believing the pain was caused from inflammation. In 1913, Dr. Luff further endorsed this name and added the correlation of other symptoms such as infections, fevers, and temperature variations to the pain of FM (rheumatology.org).

In 1965, Dr. Smythe and Dr. Moldovsky discovered disturbed sleep patterns using an EEG, which was responsible for morning stiffness, pain, fatigue, and cognition issues. In 1976 they petitioned to have the name changed to fibromyalgia since the medical field rejected the name fibrositis due to the lack of inflammation evident (rheumatology.org). In 1981, the first clinical study with significant results regarding tender points was published. In 1987, FM was recognized by the American Medical Association as a *true illness* and a cause of disability. Doctors' reluctance to accept FM as a true illness centers on the lack of clinical evidence. Sadly, FM has been called a *waste basket* illness, a *fad* disease, and a *yuppie* syndrome, which also hurts the credibility of research being performed.

In 1990, the American College of Rheumatology established the definitive criteria for diagnosing FM, which could be used initially for research purposes:

(a) Widespread pain lasting at least three months.
(b) At least eleven positive tender points out of a total possible of eighteen points.
(c) Pain lasting in all four quadrants (rheumatology.org).

In 1997, the National Fibromyalgia Association (NFA) was established and was the first national organization to advocate for FM. The main purpose of the NFA was to educate the patient about FM so that they could find a way to manage it (nfa.org).

In 2005 the first guideline for treating FM was published by the American Pain Society. The APS claims, "Fibromyalgia syndrome has no cure, is difficult to diagnose, and effective pain management strategies are a must to help patients cope with the disease" (ampainsoc.org). In 2007, the FDA approved Lyrica as the first drug to treat FM. In 2008, Cymbalta was approved by the FDA and was originally approved as a drug to treat depression. In 2009, a second anti-depressant, Savella, gained FDA approval. Other drugs are currently pending FDA approval (fda.gov). In 2010, the ACR developed a new set of criteria for diagnosing FM, which is gaining ground and raising hope, due to the nature of recognizing this illness and its many symptoms.

HOW FIBROMYALGIA IS CLASSIFIED MEDICALLY

There are many doctors, hospitals, and organizations that have placed consideration on FM in one way or another. Many of those exist as opinion, not scientific based research, and are simply incorrect. FM is one of the most misunderstood illnesses of pandemic proportions ever. Thankfully, the field of qualified experts is growing every day, but for decades, this illness has gone unrecognized for its devastating impact on the lives of so many individuals.

So who really are the experts on FM? If you consider where the most research dollars have been spent you would get one answer. If you base your conclusion on reputation, then you will get another answer. If you strictly view what the FDA and the CDC have to say about it, then you may still get another opinion. The fact is that since there are no tests that the FDA, the CDC, or most private insurance companies recognize as valid, and since there are no treatment programs that work for everyone, I think you have to become your own advocate and come to your own conclusion. If you are one of those individuals who are afflicted by the illness, decide for yourself what course of action is best for you, and then you become the expert. I think that this may become the most important thing in your life that you should know as much as you possibly can about it. In my opinion Dr. Clauw and his team at the University of Michigan School of Medicine are leading the global race on chronic pain and fibromyalgia research. In my opinion, Dr. Clauw is the most brilliant chronic pain researcher alive today and has a pure passion for his work.

Some organizations claim to be experts in FM diagnosis and treatment, so let's look at what a few of the experts are saying and consider their definitions, treatments, and outlook in general.

STANFORD UNIVERSITY

Stanford University has performed a number of clinical studies surrounding FM. Stanford states that FM is a rheumatic condition which impairs joints and soft tissue and causes chronic pain. In 2008, Stanford conducted a pain and fatigue relief clinical study using *low dose Naltrexone* which has been used for decades to treat opioid addiction. Stanford experts suggest that FM affects as much as four percent of the US population (stanford.edu).

MAYO CLINIC

You hurt all over, and you frequently feel exhausted. Even after numerous tests, your doctor can't find anything specifically wrong with you. If this sounds familiar, you may have fibromyalgia. Fibromyalgia is a chronic condition characterized by widespread pain in your muscles, ligaments, and tendons, as well as fatigue and multiple tender points—places on your body where slight pressure causes pain. Fibromyalgia occurs in about two percent of the population in the United States. Women are much more likely to develop the disorder than are men, and the risk of fibromyalgia increases with age. Fibromyalgia symptoms often begin after a physical or emotional trauma, but in many cases it appears to be that there's no triggering event (mayoclinic.com).

The Mayo Clinic's treatment protocol is to take analgesic pain meds, NSAID's, antidepressants, anti-seizure drugs, physical therapy, and counseling. They also recommend the following lifestyle changes—reduce stress, get enough sleep, exercise regularly, and maintain a healthy lifestyle. Mayo recommends complementary and alternative therapies such as: yoga, acupuncture, chiropractic care, massage therapy, self-coping and social support.

I went to the Mayo Clinic and they seem to be working hard to develop an effective FM treatment. I saw nine doctors and had twenty tests in five days and their program was the most impressive I had ever seen. At the end of day five I sat with my *consulting physician* who informed me that FM is not a disease, is not degenerative, is not disabling, and is completely manageable. I was told that with diet and exercise, I could minimize my issues, and the rest of my symptoms could be managed with pharmaceuticals, which would get me back to work.

Anyone who has FM and has read a few books or articles knows that it is not that simple. That being said, the Mayo clinic's recommendations are a very important part of your wellness process, but I would not expect to be back on your feet from disability immediately as they suggest.

THE AMERICAN COLLEGE OF RHEUMATOLOGY

The ACR was seeking a more practical criterion for diagnosing FM that did not use the tender point exam and would provide a scale for FM characteristic symptoms. One reason was to make improvements in the field, but another reason was that something like 25 percent of individuals with FM did not meet the 1990 ACR criteria, which obviously posed a problem for those people getting any kind of diagnosis, or real treatment, or Social Security benefits. In May of 2010, the ACR developed *new criteria* for FM long after their initial criteria was developed. Twenty-plus years ago, the diagnostic criteria was based on the *then* current information the medical field knew existed in FM patients-and the key here is, what they could realistically duplicate from person to person. Basically it was the only solid data they had to go by.

The new criterion involves a bit more detail and is paving the way to a quicker and more thorough diagnosis. First, the ACR decided to no longer use the tender points as the primary attribute in the definition. Second, the ACR has identified the Widespread Pain Index (WPI) as an actual quantitative measurement of FM pain. The ACR is recognizing that there are more symptoms that fit the criteria, such as fatigue, sleep disturbances, and cognitive issues, as well as an additional three points that will account for numbness, dizziness, nausea, IBS, and depression. And finally, they have begun using the Severity Scale (SS) as a qualifying measure of the FM pain and overall symptom severity (rheumatology.org).

These are wonderful improvements to the field of FM as it adds credibility to the illness, it raises the bar in diagnostic criteria, and helps to draw a thicker line between FM and all the negative connotations that surround the illness— like being a depression illness, psychosomatic, or just illegitimate. The problem still exists that even with this new criteria, roughly 12 percent of us will still not meet the criteria. The bottom line is that we now have a pain index with symptoms to diagnose FM, not just tender points, that are weak, and fluctuate over time and this is a dramatic improvement.

The ten doctors that developed the new criteria also discussed the tender points and were able to link the disorder to peripheral muscle abnormality. I would argue, however, that fibro is not out in the periphery, but originates in the brain. How ironic it is that this latter statement is made at the same time that Hong-You Ge, MD PhD of Aalborg University in Denmark, demonstrated that more than 90 percent of the predetermined eighteen tender points were actually myofascial trigger points (MTPs). This fact reinforces how I have felt about this criterion for a long time. I had asked numerous physicians about the correlation between FM and myofascial pain syndrome and have not met many who understand the relationship between the two.

So for an individual to satisfy the criteria and gain a diagnosis of FM based on the new criteria, they must fit into the following: have a WPI of seven or higher, a SS of five or higher, OR, a WPI between three to six and a SS of nine or higher. Next, these symptoms meeting those criteria scales above must also be present for at least three months. And finally, the rule of exclusion must be considered— which means you must rule out all other illnesses/diseases that mimic FM. Additionally, pain must be in all four quadrants of the body or it is not FM. It should not surprise us that at some point the issue of somatization must be considered, since almost every symptom of FM can be somatic.

The pain index is a nineteen-item checklist, where you checkoff the body parts affected by pain in the last week. And the symptom scale involves unrefreshed sleep, fatigue, and cognitive issues which are likely the three top offenders for most people after pain. The diagnosis focuses on the number of painful body parts/

areas, the number of symptoms, and finally severity. Combining the SS and the WPI allows for physicians to recommend a new case definition for FM. In the future this criterion will provide a more useful longitudinal evaluation to measure those of us with FM and variable symptoms. (Since our symptoms wax and wane, it is difficult to consistently meet the criteria).

My theory regarding this new criteria is that the number of FM patients will suddenly spike and, at least in the US, we will have a much larger demographic of FM sufferers. I think that relying on the tender point exam resulted in a serious amount of under-diagnosed men and over diagnosed women, not to mention the lack of consideration placed on the myriad other symptoms we face. This can be good in terms of research dollars being used in the field, but could stand to throw up all kinds of brick walls in other considerations, like medical and prescriptive insurance coverage, disability criteria not matching the new criteria, and so on. I think having a more concrete diagnostic criterion will significantly improve the percentage of comorbidity and especially depression in FM, as patients will be less likely to receive negativity from physicians, their families, and even society. Consideration must continue to be given to the degree of misdiagnosis moving forward.

I appreciate what the diagnosic criteria have done for us, like get FDA approved drugs and treatment protocols, but the criterion so far was very limited. As such many doctors cannot correctly diagnose FM. The tender points fluctuate, providing a basis that someone may or may not have the illness, depending on when the tender point exam is done. The 1990 criterion does not take into account ANY of the other symptoms. The 2010 criterion acts as an alternative not a replacement for it and three additional conditions must be met, including the WPI and the SS. Both of these scales can be tracked over time, and patients progress can be monitored and measured, which further supports the race for a cure.

I am pleased that we no longer will have to rely only on, in my opinion, an invalid diagnostic criterion, (tender points) which was never designed for diagnosis in the first place. (FM criteria were originally established for *classification criteria*, to be used specifically for research). Not to dwell on this issue, but I spent my entire 20's and most of my 30's searching for answers and pleading for help from the medical world and never got it until 18 years went by. I firmly propose the theory that I became sicker while my illness went on undiagnosed, untreated, and while comorbid diseases over ran my body and these perpetuating factors caused me to become totally disabled while I waited for medicine to catch up. I firmly believe that chronic pain is progressive and while I waited for answers-my illness progressed.

These organizations have similar positions on FM and I hope will grow their support in the future:

NATIONAL INSTITUTE OF HEALTH

The NIH is one of the main governmental agencies currently researching FM and helping to shape the future of medicine. There is a lot of information about FM on the NIH Website to help you learn about what they are doing to help (nih.gov).

CENTERS FOR DISEASE CONTROL AND PREVENTION

The CDC is another main governmental research agency that is spending time and money helping to make this illness more understood throughout the medical world and the advertised world as well (cdc.gov).

THE ARTHRITIS FOUNDATION

The Arthritis Foundation is the only national not-for-profit organization that supports the more than one hundred types of arthritis and related conditions. Founded in 1948, with headquarters in Atlanta, the Arthritis Foundation has multiple service points located throughout the country (arthritis.org).

After years of receiving little attention, fibromyalgia has in recent years become the focus of intense research efforts. The goal is to improve the understanding of fibromyalgia, its causes, and the problems that often accompany it in order to find better treatments and methods for prevention (arthritis.org).

Some specific areas of this research include the *family relationship*. Because fibromyalgia runs in families, researchers are trying to determine for certain whether a gene or genes predispose people to the condition. Several studies have found a possible link between genetic markers called human leukocyte antigens, or HLAs, and fibromyalgia. Although researchers are cautious about interpreting the findings, they suggest the possible existence of a predisposing gene. I strongly support the theory on genetics.

"One group of researchers is trying to determine if fibromyalgia is more common in people with other conditions, such as serious mood disorders, that tend to run in families. They are exploring whether clusters of conditions exist in families, which might shed light on shared common risk factors or disease processes" (arthritis.org).

THE AMERICAN FIBROMYALGIA SYNDROME ASSOCIATION (AFSA)

The nation's leading nonprofit organization dedicated to funding research that accelerates the pace of medical discoveries to improve the quality of life for patients with fibromyalgia.

Through donations, AFSA supports studies that seek out the causes and treatments for fibromyalgia, which is an extremely painful, fatiguing, and often debilitating medical condition that affects three to 5 percent of the population. By stepping up research on fibromyalgia, AFSA and its generous contributors are working together to make a substantial difference in the lives of millions. Scientists are currently focusing on abnormalities in the central nervous system that are believed to cause widespread muscular pain, sleep and digestive disorders, chronic headaches, memory and concentration difficulties, and many other body-wide symptoms. 90 percent of donations to AFSA go directly to fund research. The AFSA has funded over 30 projects through your generous donations (afsafund.org).

NATIONAL FIBROMYALGIA ASSOCIATION

Founded in 1997 in Orange, California, by Lynne Matallana and Karen Lee Richards, the National Fibromyalgia Association (NFA) is the largest nonprofit [501(c)3] organization working to support people with fibromyalgia and other chronic pain illnesses...after receiving non-profit status for the organization and developing a mission platform focused on executing programs to improve the quality of life for people affected by FM...The National Fibromyalgia Association became an organization made up of devoted individuals who made a concentrated effort to create a voice for people with fibromyalgia by supporting and staging awareness events, encouraging high profile media coverage, and providing support and training to support group leaders across the country. The NFA's philosophy was to help empower patients and to provide them with a new level of hope for the future...(fmaware.org).

AMERICAN CHRONIC PAIN ASSOCIATION (ACPA)

Formed in 1994 and operated by volunteers, the ACPA is a nonprofit organization dedicated to funding research for FM. (In 1994, the US government was spending less than one penny per patient on FM research). The ACPA is focusing on abnormalities in the CNS that are believed to cause many of the symptoms of FM. The ACPA claims that FM affects 3—5 percent of the population. Today, the CDC is spending millions to help push positive information about FM, which helps educate and inform the world that this is a real illness (acpa.org).

FIBROMYALGIA AND FATIGUE
CENTERS OF AMERICA

The Fibromyalgia and Fatigue Centers is the organization I am most familiar with, as I spent fourteen months as a patient there in their *Wellness Treatment Program*. They define fibromyalgia as "a complex disease in which both genetics and environmental factors play a role" (fibroandfatigue.com). They are considering the following list basic facts and symptoms about FM:

Fibromyalgia afflicts eight to twelve million people in this country alone. It does not discriminate by gender or age, although it predominately affects women between the ages of thirty-five and fifty-four. It has been found to be genetic, affecting children and the elderly, both male and female alike. Fibromyalgia is a complex disease that involves multi-system disturbances and abnormalities. Because of this complexity, these conditions have been poorly treated by the current eight to fifteen minute visits that address only a portion of the wide spectrum of underlying dysfunctions. Diagnosis is difficult. Currently there is no one medical test that will clearly diagnose fibromyalgia. Diagnosis is based on patient history and tender point sensitivity. Tender points refer to 18 points on the body in which extreme sensitivity may occur in at least eleven points. Tender point sensitivity, as well as a history of widespread chronic body pain for at least three months, provides the most definitive diagnosis at this time. Other symptoms relating to a diagnosis are listed later (fibroandfatigue. com).

This organization claims to be *the* most advanced treatment program in the US, but still only claims a 65 percent decrease in fatigue and *improvement* in pain. They verbally claim much more than they will put in writing, and the program is treated like a corporation, with a chain of command; and the doctors claim to be "just employees with no outside the box authority!"

I strongly recommend against this organization for a number of reasons. The first and most important reason is that they will likely not help you. In fact, they are likely to cause more problems than they eliminate. This is because they experiment with a science that is not yet even close to perfected, while they claim to have cornered the market on their treatment. Their scientific treatment is totally experimental and dangerous and this is the opinion of a number of physicians I had seen during and after my treatment there. I had developed more illnesses and a greater severity of existing symptoms going through their treatment, and the whole time I was complaining about becoming sicker, the staff at the clinic explained that it is normal that you will become sicker before you become well.

While this logic has its place in some treatment regimens, it falls within the scope of their experimentation and at the expense of the patient. They may occasionally stumble on an effective treatment for someone, but how would they know what that is when the majority of their patients receive the same mega doses of intravenous vitamins and minerals, and anywhere between forty to seventy pills per day. There is just no way to effectively know what is happening to your patient when you experiment in this fashion.

The second reason this clinic receives a zero in my book is cost. They charge a minimum of six thousand dollars per year, up front, and typically charge more as soon as your lab testing comes back and they determine that they can charge you more for additional treatment for viruses or neurotoxins, etc. They hook you with a promise of a cure; then bleed you dry and fix nothing!

They require you to use their pharmacy and their recommended locations for most or all of the medications you need *outside* the program, which you will come to discover are at least twice the cost versus anywhere else. They demand you use compounded mixtures for hormone replacement, which they consider *bioidentical,* which is more of a marketing term than an actual medical term. These medications typically provide no more help than any other product you would get as a generic at a standard pharmacy, plus they are extremely expensive to get them through their pharmacy. This can add up very quickly.

They recommend against exercise and suggest no special diet in particular, which is contrary to popular advice. While it is understood that with FM you will have delayed fatigue from exercise, it is still recommended that you do some sort of exercise program. And as far as diet is concerned, I will further discuss the impact of a proper diet for wellness later. But the quick answer is, you are what you eat, and with FM we are very sensitive to our nutrition.

The Fibro and Fatigue Centers took the collective intelligence of fibromyalgia wisdom and compressed it into a package so complicated that they cannot even explain it to the patient; and just ask you to pay them all of your money and just trust them to make you well again so you can regain your life. They know that by the time you have come to them, you have likely been bumped around through the medical community, and are ready for desperate measures. At this point, they blow you away with their complex scientific approach that is, of course, what no one else is doing, and convince you that it is what is working, and that they are years ahead of the competition; and subsequently why they do not take medical insurance-because they are so far advanced in their treatment program that the insurance companies have yet to catch up! After one year of treatment and you feel no change or worse, they will sell you another year of treatment and promise more and deliver less. Do your research! I personally met dozens of patients at this clinic over my fourteen months as a patient, none of whom reported any improvement to me.

WHAT THE DOCTOR'S WON'T TELL YOU

Most doctors will not tell you that they do not have the proper background to deal with FM. They will not tell you that they do not have the training in how to make a diagnosis, or what drugs to give you, besides what the FDA has approved. They will not admit if they truly believe in the illness or not, and some certainly will not hesitate to point out to you how your lifestyle has likely caused your illness.

I am not sure if pride or arrogance is their driving force that makes them dangerous, or if they have so little respect for FM that they will make broad, generalized swats at it until they can think of someone to refer you to. Find the right clinicians. Always ask for a copy of your medical records so you can assemble your own packet for when you need access to information, especially the *doctor's notes* section of your file. You may need to prepare for your next visit and you may want to disregard the derogatory doctor notes from your last visit if your physician is not supportive. Often, doctors, who are not psychologists, will add psychological notes in your file about your attitude, demeanor, or personality; and depending on their personal beliefs on FM, their remarks may negatively impact the future of your care. All it takes is for one physician to label you a hypochondriac, or depressive or that you are *just seeking pills* to make it very difficult for you to be taken seriously in the future, and even more difficult to obtain disability income where possible.

FROM DEFEAT TO ACCEPTANCE

Chronic illness comes like a thief in the night who takes what he can when he can, starting with the difficult to miss stuff. In order to get moving some days often you may have to psych yourself out like someone who is getting ready to jump out of an airplane or into a cold lake. When FM is at its worst, every moment of your waking day can be consumed by defeat. From the time you wake, you are already planning your priorities according to each day's start, since each day is unpredictably different from one another. One major component of my wellness was controlling my schedule, which allowed me to remain somewhat in control of my environment—and pacing becomes critical. In fact pacing is the single easiest thing you can do to manage your worst flares.

Receiving the news that you have fibromyalgia. When you receive the news that you have fibromyalgia, typically for many of us that comes with baggage. We may already have a predisposed opinion and knowledge about fibro, the same way we have a predisposed knowledge about cancer. If we are told today that we have cancer, our reaction almost immediately makes us feel worse. The suggestion of illness carries with it a negative connotation that impacts our symptom expression and depending on how equipped we are to handle the news of impending illness, our resilience will depend on how the initial and ongoing impact will be on our overall well-being.

Another example of this put simply is this: If you were bitten by a snake and you had no idea what kind of snake it was, your first reaction may be to panic and fear death and other terrible things. But if you knew that you were bitten by a non-venomous garter snake, your brain would likely *understand* the ramifications of the incident and you would react accordingly, which is to say your brain would not put your body on high alert, fight-or-flight mode, making all of your bodily systems go crazy—this stress impact would boost your pain. Your reaction to your innocent snake bite will be totally minimized by your brains prior experience and *knowledge* with everything you know about a non-venomous snake bite-which is not to over react.

I realize that finding out about fibro carries with it more of an impact than a non-venomous snake bite, but the idea is the same-depending on how your brain is developed to react, will determine to what degree your illness gets the best of you. Another example would be an oncologist developing cancer. Who better to deal with a cancer diagnosis than a cancer doctor? His knowledge will not cure him, but it will set the scene for how he will initially react to the news, how he will approach treatment and therapy, how quickly he accepts his situation, and how he views his life after accepting his illness.

Most of us are not totally educated about fibro before it strikes like an oncologist is about cancer, which is ok. Most everyone in the world knows what cancer is, but that does not mean they are not going to learn as much as they can once they face it. The knowledgeable patient will be the more successful patient. Knowledge about fibro will be the difference between bad symptoms or worse symptoms.

Another example of understanding your situation is your career. We attempt to learn as much as we can about our job, and maybe we take it a bit further and learn everything we can about the company as a whole, so that we can get our arms around our environment and perform at our best. When you are ill, you should want to become good at it like it was your job and a promotion depended on it-or your life depended on it! You learn everything about it and you impress your physicians, just like you would impress your bosses, and before you know it you are really qualified to manage your illness, and by default you are controlling your symptoms to a high degree. You own your pain. You can choose to be in control of your pain through knowledge and understanding.

In the beginning, when you first are learning to cope with FM, you have to use your whole arsenal to get you to the point of managing your illness. This is something no one else will be able to do for you. People will be able to help you to a point, but you have to have the will to get well, and you have to accept your illness before you can do that.

You have to treat every day as an opportunity to compete against yourself. Your performance will vary dramatically, and so will your results. You have to set goals and objectives that are reachable today, not yesterday, keeping in mind that you are not the same person you used to be. This is where the struggles come in to play, and this is why you have to *accept* who you are today. Everyone is different, but most who suffer from FM will perform short of their expectations. This is okay. This is often a process to get used to. No one likes when things are taken from them, especially when they are physical abilities, and this illness *can* take from you. Our gift is in our strength to cope with the losses associated with chronic illness. Throughout history, humans have proven again and again that we have the survival skills necessary to push forward under any circumstances and I find comfort in knowing that it could always be worse.

No matter the tragedy or illness, there is a degree of acceptance we must go through, and that includes our family and friends, if you plan to keep them in your life. The sooner you can adjust your attitude to accept the changes that are occurring in your life the better you will cope, and the better you will *allow* those around you to cope.

It is okay to feel defeated, *sometimes*, as long as you can accept that defeat is not the end. If you do not have something to hope for and look forward to then find something. Continue to search for a slice of motivation to get you through each day; sometimes that is what it takes. Along the way, you are assembling a team of clinicians that will support you through the difficult road ahead. Eventually you have to quit focusing on your misery, because misery is a slippery slope that will consume you and add to your symptoms.

Being challenged by so many things it is hard to find common ground for accomplishments, pride, fun, and happiness, but somehow we do it. Success does not have to be a thing of the past, neither does fun nor having a social life. With fibro, you create your success. You do not have to become your worst fears. This illness is not who you are and it does not define you, unless you let it. You have to look to your spouse or family for strength and hope initially, until you learn how to look to yourself for strength and hope. Consider rebooting your thinking with some hope. Your reality can become skewed to your perception of yourself if you allow it to. It can become a cycle of negativity that has its own direction and set of goals. Sometimes you still have to create a logical argument from those emotions, and you will find that eventually, it is enough.

FIBROMYALALGIA— ACCEPTANCE AND COPING

Someone recently asked me, "What if I never feel any better? What if my fibro symptoms never go away? I have already faced so much pain, so much loss. Help me understand how I am supposed to be okay with this, to move on with this, to accept this? Tell me how I move on from here?" I think at some point in our illness, we all ask questions like these. There is no easy answer. I find comfort in knowing that we are not alone in this, and that there are many people just like us, in the same situation, and I am constantly reminded that it could always be worse.

Chronic illness is very complex and so is learning to accept and live with it. It can take a long time to become accustomed to life after disease. Your attitude has a great deal to do with your coping and recovery. The way you view your situation translates into your symptom expression and how you view managing your health from here on out. If you view the glass half empty, if you remain pessimistic, and if you approach your treatment with negativity, then you will have a much harder and longer road to recovery. Manage your health to the best of your ability. Keep a positive attitude. Do not give up hope, and I guarantee you will feel better.

LOOKING FOR HOPE

"Once you choose hope, anything is possible."

—Christopher Reeve

I think it really does come down to making a choice. I would like to believe that once you are able to get your arms around hope, you can control your fears a little bit more. It is almost poetic how hope may be one of the most unstoppable words in the world. It is powerful at any level, and I sometimes wonder, without hope what else would we have to get us through the tough times?

"The road that is built in hope is more pleasant to the traveler than the road built in despair, even though they both lead to the same destination."

—Marian Zimmer Bradley

Chronic illness will challenge you every day, and those equipped to handle it will better succeed than those who are not, than those who look to illness, to pain, and to sadness without hope, and those who refuse to let hope into their hearts.

"Hope is the feeling we have that the feeling we have is not permanent."

—Mignon McLaughlin

Very little in this life is permanent. We chronic pain sufferers are left to feel hopeless at times. We often wonder if what we are going through actually can last forever. Our minds have the ability to transform bad into good, ugly into beautiful, and hopeless into hopeful. Our attitudes require constant attention to maintain a system of checks and balances, and most people have a different path that takes them to the same place. Ours may be more difficult than some, but easier than others.

Hope can become toxic, and like our many symptoms, can be fed by other negative thoughts. Hope can be a job, while anything else can be easier. I think hope is an emotion that is independent but is influenced by everything. Without hope we are susceptible to more pain and loss, and hope has deceived many people before you.

> "Hope never abandons you, you abandon it."
>
> —George Weinberg

Hope is a commitment of the soul. It allows us to get up when we are down, to win when we are losing, and to live when we are dying. Hope may be God's greatest medicine, and it comes in many forms. We can demand that our hope is an endless hope, versus a hopeless end, and strength will grow from this virtue.

> "Learn from yesterday, live for today, and hope for tomorrow."
>
> —Albert Einstein

Our success is based on our ability to adapt to our needs, and our needs change from day to day, and so must our hope. In the midst of our pain, we can discover an invincible hope. We need to seek what is beyond our hope, and that will destroy any toxic pessimism that exists within our present.

> "To find what you seek in the road of life, the best proverb of all is that which says: Leave no stone unturned."
>
> —Edward Bulwer Lytton

There is great value in a rigid attempt at what you want. Your pursuit for health is no different. We are taught to put the laws of medicine in the hands of physicians and our faith in God. We have to be willing to accept that it is up to us to find what we seek on our own, and with the assistance of those in the medical field. We have to depend on ourselves to a higher degree than we do others, and through education, we can achieve a victory here.

THE POWER OF HOPE, ATTITUDE, AND SUGGESTION

Sometimes hope may seem out of reach. It may seem impossible, and it may seem like a dark reality. It is at this time that we must see the beauty of hope through the fog of pain. Our willingness to press on is our ambition of hope. Hoping for the best, but preparing for the worst is a virtue that serves us well. The chronic nature of our symptoms is like a mask in the darkness, but our education serves as our weapons against adversity. Some days I could not find my hope, and some days hope was all I had. I realized that many days I robbed myself of the single greatest tool in my arsenal. One that would burn like an eternal flame and that could be as strong as the richest faith. You can be defeated over and over again; God only knows that is part of the game. But defeat cannot take away your hope.

How you interpret your pain translates into how you experience your pain. Thinking positively can often result in you feeling better. When you live with chronic pain, often you have catastrophic thoughts and those thoughts can become toxic. Your first thoughts of the day are generally those that accompany you for hours; and since you likely awaken feeling exhausted, fluish and in pain, your thoughts immediately impact your attitude—possibly for the whole day.

One moment of weakness upon awakening ruins your whole day. Catastrophic thinking like this affects your pain. You may arrive at the mind-set that you are incapable of doing certain activities, or maybe being around certain crowds due to the disability of your illness. As soon as you begin to withdraw from life, quitting becomes that much easier and you will be full of regret. Your illness does not define you and it certainly does not make predictions about what you will be able to accomplish going forward.

Totally disabled individuals have accomplished amazing things, certainly not because their inabilities stood in their way. Ask yourself, what you want to do today and make a plan to do it. It may feel fitting to create labels for your condition(s) to suit your perception of your lifestyle but as soon as you do, you further back yourself into a corner. When you have chronic pain it is suggested that your perception of pain can become negative, distorted, and even exaggerated. It can be of great value to you if you can minimize your symptoms with a strong attitude or perception of them.

LEARNING TO COPE

I think it is important that you read and understand the next line I have written. You may have to face the fact that you are partly responsible for your condition, and going forward you certainly are responsible for your illness. A virus or genetics may have started the pot cooking, but you may have brought it to a boil with poor nutrition, stress, the lack of exercise, poor sleep hygiene, and flat out over doing it too much and for too long. Your body may need a hard reboot which can be difficult when you have FM.

Then there is the fact that you may have been sick for a long time, with no treatment, or the wrong treatment. This is where my opinion differs slightly from what is accepted in the medical field. If you have a severe level of FM, then you have likely gone from infection or injury-to very sick, and depending on how you react, you may become severely *deconditioned*, which can seem like degeneration. This illness affects everyone so differently, even with similar symptoms. So many things perpetuate or exacerbate FM, and so many illnesses fall into the comorbid category surrounding FM that it is just too much of a coincidence that everything is unrelated. So, I theorize that if you did not aggressively attack a treatment plan, understandably so and if you did not take care of yourself through diet and exercise then I think your FM can appear degenerative, and have deconditioned you to a point of terrible health. You can have many more symptoms and much more severity than someone who approaches the illness from a much stronger angle and a higher degree of attitude and will power. Thus, you greet your clinicians with a severely complex case to solve. Again, this is understandable since you have likely been rejected by the medical field and found no answers for so long that you may have just given up at some point and thrown in the towel. Well now it is time to pick up the pieces.

Acceptance is a major part of any healing process, and the sooner you accept where you stand right now, the better off you will be going forward. I also feel that it is important to understand and accept how you arrived here. Addressing all hidden or causative issues is helpful to your psychology, and since medicine will only take you so far in this battle, facing your past from a psychological standpoint helps to get closure to potentially unpleasant chapters in your life. Essentially, you are just telling yourself the whole story and not allowing yourself to deny any aspect of your health history as *relevant* in your recovery plan. It is very easy to lie to yourself, and it is even easier to deny some small detail in your life that may be detrimental to your wellness. Be honest with yourself. If your past distresses you, then your illness will seem worse. Address your stress and reverse some of your symptoms.

If you are anything like me, you have been a quitter more than one time in the development of your understanding of your illness. I have quit more times than I could ever count, mostly because I have been defeated more times than I can count by pain and fatigue and loss and negative physicians and failure in general. And my job has kicked my ass many times over the years, and I felt as though there was nothing I could do about it. Like the quit smoking ads say, "You can't quit quitting" and that goes quadruple for FM. It takes a firm hold on your present state and the right attitude to stay in the game.

My life was full of shortcomings and apologies and I always struggled to get past illness-related failures. You did not choose to be sick but you can choose to have a champion attitude about your recovery, and you can choose what you do with what you are given. With each new or worsening symptom or setback, I would have to readjust to the changes, increase my current confidence level and find a new acceptance. On any given day I would go from fatigued and functional to bedridden. At times social isolation would get the better of me as I felt I was forced to change and hated that fact that anything in my life could be so out of control. I realized that I had to change the way I thought about pain and deal with the illness more positively, and that there was more to attitude and perspective than I ever anticipated.

Another coping strategy that is shown to provide benefit is controlled breathing. Breathing techniques have proven to be a useful tool to eliminate and control pain and nausea and further to bring you into a relaxed state before, during, or after stressful events or activities arise. Focused breathing in through your nose and directing the inhalation into your stomach versus into your chest, and then exhaling through your mouth as if you were gently fogging up a mirror with your breath allows for a deeper, more focused and relaxed technique of breathing that can provide symptom relief for some people. Mastering this one technique is just the beginning of you reclaiming control of your life.

PSYCHOLOGY OF FIBROMYALGIA

A percentage of FM sufferers will develop some degree of depression. Consequently, the percentage of those who will get depression will not be any higher than individuals who suffer from other types of chronic illness. Typically, psychological disorders like depression or anxiety arise out of the mind's inability to effectively deal with chronic illness. Fibro symptoms are suggested to be impacted by our behaviors, our psychology, and our cognition. In depression, heredity can be a factor, but so can the lack of exercise, poor nutrition, and the ability to relax oneself (which can affect us at the chemical level).

Your problems may begin to stack up on you. Eliminating stressors are effective in reducing fatigue, headaches, and so on. It is hard not to be stressed out when many of us feel like we are in the fight of our lives some days, but it is possible, especially one step at a time. Forget who you used to be or how easy things came to you before you became ill. Essentially you are the same person but with new equipment and a new instructional manual. Often you will find that you become frustrated by your inability to *do* what you used to easily be able to do. This is counterproductive and will cause setbacks in your recovery. Remember, no one can do this for you; you have to hope for the best and that has to be part of your focus for recovery, and that you will slowly regain physical and mental characteristics. That is the best thing about this illness is that you can reverse it.

That is where the biggest slice of optimism slides into place. You can be in control of winning or losing this race. You have to equip yourself with the education, tools, and support, and keep your eye on the prize. Your biggest obstacle will be your attitude, keeping in mind how slippery slopes are easy to fall into. Do not focus on the nonbelievers, especially the doctors. Whether or not you are depressed, finding a good therapist can be a big help to your recovery. A therapist can also be your best advocate as they can relate to your condition and the psychological impact it can have on you from the start. Cognitive behavioral therapy (CBT) is very valuable for FM wellness.

At some point you will get your diagnosis, and maybe you are diagnosed with numerous illnesses, conditions, or syndromes. For many people, all of their symptoms, believe it or not, still fall under the fibro umbrella. It is always a relief for me to receive the information that I have something tangible that I can at least know is contributing to my poor health. As I have said previously, education is such an important fundamental building block in your recovery, and knowing exactly what you have and do not have helps you move forward. A good rheumatologist will know if your symptoms belong to fibro or are seperate illnesses. Once you get past the diagnosis stage of the illness, you will feel like things are truly moving forward and if you remember back to before you received a diagnosis—everything seemed to be on hold.

Another consideration that needs to be addressed is your ability to maintain relationships. Losing friends can be a part of this illness because you are just too tired to remain social and keep in touch with others. I make an attempt to reach out as often as I can and that peels back the dark cloud a little bit. In the beginning all you want to do is have those you know understand that you are going through something significant and that their expectations of you should be reduced while you are sick. It took me years to be able to say no to my friends who asked me for favors like to help them move or even to help them with their resume. I felt like I was in my own version of the *Twilight Zone*, which isolated me even more, and caused setbacks.

I wanted people to know I had FM, but I did not want to tell them. I did not want to have to say, "I have fibromyalgia! Yes it is that illness that makes you extra tired and in pain. Yes it is so bad I cannot work right now. No, there is not really anything that treats it effectively today." I was always embarrassed to even talk about it at all, because it was so misunderstood. I even hated for my relatives to know because no one takes the time to learn what it really does to you, and then assumptions begin and suddenly you are the family black sheep, who must be lazy and depressed!

In the last few years though, it seems like a revolution began at some point and created a chain reaction in the FM world. I would like to say that it hit the world like an explosion, but it didn't, it was subtle. But FM is slowly gaining forward momentum and I think soon enough it will be as valid as many of the other tragic diseases of the twenty-first century, once thought to be just as invalid as FM like depression, polio, lupus, MS, Parkinson's, Lyme's disease, Gulf War Syndrome, and many more. Once in a while you may even see a commercial about FM on TV, bringing hope and credibility to the illness. And the pharmaceutical companies are doing their part too.

As much as I would like to separate depression from fibro, I think it is important to make a distinction. Depression can be a valid and significant part of FM for many people and needs to be taken more seriously than most of the symptoms associated with the illness. While depression can be effectively treated with therapy or medication, or biofeedback or lifestyle changes, or a combination of the above, it is easy to miss the signs and continue trying to live a normal life untreated, denying the truth.

Often the symptoms of FM mimic other illnesses. Sometimes the signs of depression mimic FM closely as well. As part of your action recovery plan, you should be keeping some kind of journal or written testament of your symptoms for a few reasons, but mainly because identifying secondary illnesses like depression is critical. Some of the more obvious signs to look for are: feeling helpless, hopeless, sadder than normal, self-loathing, worthless, and wanting to die. Some of the more subtle signs are feeling agitated, restless, irritable, fatigued, sleepy, drained, guilty, or on edge. If you have sudden weight changes, are uninterested in activities, do not want to be social, have cognition issues and have aches and pains these could also be signs of depression. As I said previously, many of these signs resemble the symptoms of FM so it takes some evaluation to know what is going on, and your primary care physician may not be capable of recognizing these symptoms compared to physical illnesses.

I feel like I would not be thorough if I did not explain that it is pretty normal to be depressed when you have a chronic illness-to a degree. You should feel depressed or sad about the pain you are in, about the loss you have faced, about the challenges you go through every day, and about the financial difficulties you may face with FM, etc. If you didn't, I would say you are exceptionally strong or even weird. It is a fairly natural reaction to a painful outcome. But there is a difference between depression from circumstances in life and the clinical illness that I am referring to, that benefits from talk therapy or medication.

It is believed that there is an increased risk for suicide in those people suffering with chronic pain. FM is not so commonly publicized in this category. When you consider a disease like FM that is so misunderstood and further disregarded by the medical community or even your family and friends, it makes sense that it could easily fit into this category. Suffering with FM already makes you feel like you are many things, and isolated can quickly become another one. The patient's emotions can also quickly become tangled and their needs are typically far from met. We are in pain, we are fatigued, we have ten other symptoms, and no one understands! We have seen eight doctors this year and none of them have helped. We have run out of money. We are too sick to work, and we are worried about how we are going to make it through the next month. Our lives can seem hopeless fast. Now factor depression in!

Early on in the illness, like many other illnesses, you may be in denial. Denial is a temporary defense, typically followed by some degree of acceptance. Some people cannot handle the truth, possibly because it breaks down denial. Others use denial extensively in many aspects of their lives. What can be worse is that you may encounter negativity or doubt from those around you, especially those in the medical field, and that can be devastating. Depression can make your symptoms seem exaggerated sometimes, drawing a heavier focus toward a psychological disorder and away from fibromyalgia, blurring your diagnosis. Often there is a grieving process that goes along with chronic pain. And sadly, emotional issues like depression often are not a covered medical benefit—so we go on without help. The process of reaching an acceptance stage of the illness is not unlike the grieving of a lost loved one. If you are not able to successfully transition through these stages of grieving and accept your illness and how it has impacted you, psychological disorders like depression and anxiety can develop.

Negative thoughts are important and often result in depression, but worst of all for those of us who struggle with lifelong chronic illness, negative thoughts often become distorted and lead to catastrophizing (catastrophic thinking). An example of catastrophic thinking would be saying, "I am so sick right now, I will never feel better." You have to challenge these thoughts. CBT is a useful tool to teach you how to do this.

Depression often leads to poor diet, lack of exercise, poor hygiene, and can exacerbate your chronic illness symptoms. Whereas, laughter on the other hand relaxes the muscles, changes breathing patterns, increases blood circulation, and stimulates the immune system, as well as taking your mind off the pain.

Pain relief can involve temporarily leaving the here and now and taking your mind elsewhere. Visualization is similar to a state of relaxation. You visualize the painful parts of your body, confronting it, and reducing it to a manageable thing. Try this: picture a warm waterfall flowing downward. Now picture you are lying under the waterfall and the warmth of the water is soothing all of your muscle pain. Allow the water to focus on your worst pain. It brings comfort. Allow the water to provide relief. Allow the pain to become the water, flowing, deeper and deeper until you can no longer feel the pain. Sometimes it just takes, taking your mind off the pain. I have experienced many approaches to wellness and I can say with absolute certainty that I prefer and support a psychological approach. Psychology is a soft science and people are mostly soft, and ambiguities about chronic illness are also soft versus western medicine *hard science*. This is why I feel that knowledge, attitude, and self-management (psychological perspectives) are your best defense against fibro.

IS IT OKAY TO IGNORE YOUR ILNESS

I think it is common to have your emotions wax and wane like your symptoms, with regard to denial and acceptance of illness. Even after you come to terms with your illness, you can experience periods of hopelessness, trial and error therapies, or just plain give up trying at times.

The common end result is depression, isolation, taking it out on others, or anger. Being well versed in your illness will help you to avoid the deep depression, mood swings, and setbacks that are common with these periods. Ignoring your illness is denying that it exists and is counter-productive to wellness.

You need to find and use the tools that constantly deliver you to acceptance and allow you to choose positive actions to combat negativity. Reversing anger is possible-really it is more like using anger effectively to transition to the next step which is often bargaining. Bargaining can be a depressing, fearful, and anxious time. We all ask why me, again and again. I prefer to be in the right frame of mind as often as possible so that I can positively or constructively answer myself when I ask that question. I find comfort in knowing that I am not alone, that there are systems of support to help me move forward, and that there is always someone suffering more than I am which gives me strength to push on.

Eventually most of us accept. It is hard not to and it is human nature to accept the life we have been given. Dark clouds have a way of settling on us as well as lifting from us. We can train ourselves to lift the cloud through dozens of interventions and techniques like CBT— even if our illness is so bad that we must rebuild our lives, only after facing loss after painful loss. We simply pick up the pieces and reinvent ourselves. We stop looking backwards, we accept, and we stop being the victim. We live our lives one day at a time. We face one failure at a time. And we aim for one victory at a time.

WHAT CAN ATTITUDE DO FOR YOUR ILLNESS?

Before I developed chronic illness, I could do one hundred things and twenty of those things well. Today I can do eighty-five things and ten of them well. Chronic illness did not get the best of me, and I do not focus on the fifteen things I cannot do anymore. In fact, I can do a few new things I never thought I could like be patient, proactive, compassionate, mindful, to slow down, to learn to live with less, to become spiritual, to find satisfaction in the little things, and to appreciate the many opportunities life has presented to me. I am still in charge of my life—how I act, react, and what I allow to affect me or get me down. I have so much today I cannot imagine wasting any of my time on what I do not have or cannot do.

So where would I be today without the will to be well and a strong attitude? A few years ago I allowed my illness to defeat me and I found that I surrendered to it almost completely and I began to withdraw from life one activity at a time. My illness was a prison and I was a victim. With that withdrawal I began to experience the loss associated with chronic illness, most of which I was in control of but did not realize it at the time.

After much soul searching and years of introspection, I decided it was time to rejoin my life and begin moving forward again. I loaded my schedule up with wishes and desires which slowly turned into actions. I buried myself in positive activities that I knew would translate into positive habits that would promote wellness.

I decided to no longer be the victim and began making and keeping commitments. I decided it was time to start making promises again, which for a long time I could not keep. I committed to an exercise regimen, which some days would break me and other days it made me stronger. I slowly began to see that with the right attitude and the will to beat my illness, I could make positive gains which raised the dark cloud a little at a time and slowly began to reverse my fibromyalgia.

I realized that I needed to make significant changes in my life in order to rejoin my life. I decided to get a PhD in psychology so that I could continue to work and not be a drain on society, since I could no longer perform my previous job, and also so that I could pay it forward where possible and help others with fibromyalgia. I volunteer with organizations dedicated to advancing fibromyalgia, which gave me purpose and allowed me to promote fibromyalgia awareness. Consider this: What has been most important in my path to wellness has been attitude. What can you achieve with the right attitude?

COUNSELING THOSE WITH CHRONIC ILLNESS

Research has shown that psychological factors play a large role in how patients experience and express pain. Patients need to understand that they can play a role in fixing a large part of their problem by partnering with their clinicians. It has become typical to see an interdisciplinary treatment protocol allowing patients the tools needed to help themselves function and cope. It has been determined that using self-help programs with a counselor was more effective than self-help by itself.

Chronic pain therapy is more effective with an interdisciplinary approach involving medication only where needed. Chronic pain patients have often suffered trauma, sexual and physical abuse, fear avoidance, and anxiety. Patients suffering from chronic pain often realize pain that is disproportionate to their trauma or injury and are typically unsuccessful with treatment until they come to terms with their emotions.

WHAT IT REALLY TAKES

You need to get to a point that you feel okay doing almost nothing, before you start doing activities that cause you to cycle or flare. There are specific actions you can take that are within your control and your control only; no one can do these things for you, and it starts with a plan. Once you create a recovery action plan or wellness plan, you have to succumb to a lifestyle that may include a huge list of aids like tools for memory, tools for physical motion, the right doctors, the right fitness plan, the right sleep, the right diet, the right support staff and family, and most of all an attitude adjustment. Keep your eye on the prize.

Your plan should start with educating yourself and keeping track of your illness. Know what you are up against and know how to illustrate that to your health team. Assembling your health team can be difficult and can take time. Typically, rheumatologists are the most qualified to diagnose FM, and further treat it and advocate for you in the event you need to seek disability. A neurologist is equally qualified to help you, especially addressing the issue of pain, but I would still recommend starting with a rheumatologist. You may also want to work with your family physician for the basics and prescription refills and for someone to hold all of your records in one place. There are also physiatrists, pain specialists, and physical therapists that can be effective members of your team. A combination of evolving medications, significant nutritional changes, cognitive behavioral therapy, and a re-evaluated lifestyle will be finishing touches to assembling your health team.

Sleep becomes critically important in your treatment regimen. Without proper sleep, and a good sleep schedule, you will exacerbate many of your symptoms. Nutrition is important in general health and in most diseases. Since FM is a disease characterized by fatigue, it just makes sense that you need the right fuel for the engine, despite there being no medically suggested diet for FM currently. Most people with FM do not fully respond to the first medication or treatment they try. That being said, it is important to try as many treatments as are necessary until you find relief; which may mean numerous attempts in numerous directions—the complementary approach.

You may have to plan on changing who you are to get yourself out of the rut you are in. Who you are today has everything to do with where you are today. And likely who you were yesterday, will not be who you are tomorrow because this illness is going to force changes in you. The more you educate yourself, the more you will be prepared for the changes as they come, or go. Without change, something sleeps inside us. It may be time to redefine what you can and cannot do, before what you cannot do redefines you.

HOW DO I DEAL WITH DISEASE?

I talk to numerous people with fibromyalgia and more than a few have commented on the lifestyle I lead and my disease management approach. They asked, "How do you get through every day and stay positive? How do you beat depression? How do you motivate yourself to push through the pain, day after day? How does life go on with fibro?"

It's not that the answer is simple, its not, its complex, but I committed to it and so far it has been the one thing keeping me from being totally disabled, and totally depressed. I decided many years ago that I needed a strategy for my disease(s), I needed a wellness plan, I needed a schedule, and I needed a number of things I could control in order to manage my illness. I also needed to commit to specific treatment interventions or it would all be for nothing. Finally, I needed to address my sleep hygiene.

This took me many months to achieve. I wanted to quit several times—don't quit.

- My strategy was to beat my illness.

- My wellness plan was a broad group of clinicians, of which I manage the whole program.

- My schedule was a complex paradigm of activities, sleep, rest, and actions, etc.

- My controlling items were: sleep hygiene, nutrition, fitness, stress control, alone time, stopping bad habits, eliminating negative influences, forming new healthy habits, and cautious pacing.

- My treatment interventions became: assembling my clinical team according to my needs and based on my research, determining my necessary medications and my optional supplements and CBT. Developing my fitness program, and my nutritional approach. My private time included: meditation, music, self-hypnosis, controlled breathing, and simple pleasures in life.

- I suggest championing your sleep hygiene program. If you do not have one, learn how to get one. The lack of sleep you are missing is significantly impacting your symptoms and exacerbating your illness. That is it. That is how you live with chronic illness. That is the basic shell of what it takes to manage your illness, something your clinicians will not do for you. Oh, and you have to accept your illness before you begin, you have to accept what has happened to you, and you have to adjust your attitude and conform to the following: you learn to educate yourself and advocate for yourself; you learn to stop being the victim; you are not dying, stop catastrophizing; and even if you are dying it can be addressed with dignity and acceptance; you have to be willing to change your lifestyle; you have to turn your weaknesses into you strengths; you have to allow the dark cloud to lift; you have to learn to replace negative thought with positive ones; you get to acceptance and that can be the healthiest thing you can do for yourself; you learn actions you can take today that will improve your situation and you learn to stop negative behaviors and start positive behaviors that turn into habits; you learn that seeing a psychologist for cognitive behavioral therapy to develop new and better ways to cope with the changing dynamics brought on by the illness is also beneficial; and finally, you learn to rejoin your life.

I used to be a whole lot of things I was happy about, I was proud of, and I was committed to. I have not forgotten what those things were, but I have learned to replace those things with new things, things that fill those holes, things that bring me joy, different things from what I did before I got sick. I am a different person today—not worse—I am more passionate, I am more patient, I am more understanding, I volunteer my time every moment possible to help me create positive actions in my life that will help to make me whole again.

I reached a point in my life that it had occurred to me that having numerous illnesses, the sum of which disable me physically some days, has become a *gift*. In all my pain, in all my suffering, in all my shortcomings, I still feel that I have received a gift. Every one of us with chronic illness can experience this gift, and then we have to decide what we are going to do with it. There is nothing in the world like paying it forward—sharing the positive pieces you have learned about your disease with those who have not yet arrived there.

Everything I have discussed has happened to me and many others. If you have not arrived there yet then read this again and figure out how to get these things. I am not selling anything here-this is a lifestyle choice you have to make and commit to and again—*no one* can do it for you. It is all on you. You own your wellness, you take your steps in the right direction, and you manage your health, not your clinicians. They will only deliver you to a degree of freedom from illness. The rest is up to you.

At the end of the day you may still be in pain, you still may be tired, and you still may have many of the same symptoms. I am not telling you how to eliminate your symptoms, because most of us cannot eliminate most of our symptoms. I am telling you how reduce them and to cope with living *with* them. People do it every day and have for hundreds of years before you. It is possible. You face your pain head on and address these issues above, and you keep addressing them over and over again. Maybe your symptoms will not go away. So you equip yourself and cope.

Then what? Then you mix up your program and try again. You dig deep down and find the strength to do it again. You do not quit because quitting means everything will get worse, you symptoms, your relationships, your job; your physicians will know you are getting lazy in your program and are no longer managing your illness and they will stop partnering with you. Sick or not, you are still in control of your life and if you cannot afford for it to fall apart then don't let it. You reach down as deep as necessary and find the strength to stay one step ahead of your disease.

I challenge you to take a trip somewhere where there are severely disabled individuals, individuals without limbs, or terminal individuals. And you take a hard look in the mirror and you assess your situation, and then you assess their situation. There is always someone who has life much harder than you, and many of them *live* their lives to the fullest. That is what you are going to do from this moment on. You are going to live your life to the fullest. Figure out how.

Human resilience, the will to live, and above all, attitude in the face of chronic illness is the goal. Most of us are exposed to some kind of loss, trauma, or injury throughout our lives, and some are exposed to chronic illness. A percentage of those suffering from chronic illness are able to maintain a positive attitude and hope despite pain, and loss, and suffering. The psychological impact of ineffectively coping can be overwhelming. Maintaining hope can minimize disability and loss of function.

So what is it that makes some people resilient and stronger than others with the same illness, the same opportunities in life, and the same potentially poor outlook on their health? It's a fact that everyone deals with events like living with chronic illness differently. Some may experience a minor event and face a lifetime of results, like pain symptoms. Some people continue to face serious events throughout their lives, and are able to lead fairly normal, productive lives with strong coping skills.

Positive actions in coping can be beneficial to those who have experienced a psychological impact caused by chronic illness. Talking about and thus working through the negative thoughts and impact of the illness can be effective. The *will to live* is an expression that translates into significant meaning. It can improve the quality of life for many. Humans have a fierce instinct for survival-and that puts fight in our game, and raises our will to live.

This is not to say that sometimes our biology will be impacted so severely that we cannot control our will to live much more than we can control our disease. However, it is our *attitude* that dictates our coping response and thus our success at navigating through our illness.

Our attitude also helps determine to what extent we will respond to therapy, and for how long we continue to positively respond to therapy, in the face of a complex, myriad symptoms, that for most of us *does not* end in death. Most diseases are not curable, and the treatments for many more are not favorable for a large number of patients. What does this leave for the rest of us? The hard reality for many who suffer from chronic illness rests in the theory of resilience, attitude, and the will to live. I do not draw a line between the end result of the psychological and the physical impact as a whole. Treating the body as a whole is not a new concept in medicine, but it may be unfamiliar to many physicians today. I think many of the illnesses that do not have cures and do not respond well to treatment must be approached with a complimentary approach.

We have reached an era in medicine where the psychological and physical elements of the body are considered one. They are combined, related, and linked in every way imaginable. Wellness, then, is the result of a balance between the physical, emotional, psychological, and the nutritional aspects of humans. Therapeutic interventions such as cognitive behavioral therapy, meditation, hypnosis, guided imagery, biofeedback, acupuncture, massage, breathing techniques, and yoga are becoming commonplace in the treatment of chronic illness; and let's not to forget attitude as a powerful modality for symptom relief.

It is no secret that the minds ability to work with the body toward wellness has been heavily debated scientifically. That is okay, because you may want to try what is recommended by mainstream medicine first, before you resort to outside the box thinking, when you have an illness of significance. My personal approach to my debilitating chronic illness is that I wake up every day and challenge myself to attain everything I want to. I *only* take steps in positive directions, and transcend as if nothing was wrong. I am not ignoring the fact that I have numerous problems and symptoms that so far, do not respond well to treatment, but it is those exact reasons that I decide to push on each day. I do not know how it is going to work out. I do not know how it will all end. That does not matter to me, because I did not know those things before I got sick, and I am certainly not going to let those things cripple or kill me, simply because I could not get my attitude right.

Elisabeth Kubler-Ross developed the five stages of grief which describe the five psychological stages we are likely to go through in the event of a death, disaster, injury, or illness, etc.

This model suggests that most humans *will* be able to decide to assess their *new* reality and move on, eventually accepting their situation. This is scientifically proven after decades of research.

Having the will to live means making a decision to move on, to live life to the fullest, and to find ways to make yourself happy, even if it is not the life you would have chosen for yourself otherwise. You do not have to let your illness paralyze you. There are a *thousand hope generators* out there and any one can enhance your will to live. Finding hope is your responsibility, no one can do it for you. You have to decide to want something more for yourself than illness. A strong hope can increase your ability to cope, and that nurtures the will to live. If I sometimes sound like a broken record then good, the more you hear these ideas, the more likely they are to sink in.

At some point you make the move from helpless victim to advocate in charge of your future. You are in charge of setting the tone for friends and family around you to follow as well. As you learn to live with sickness, you slowly realize change. Your *coping readiness* determines how long your particular transition will take and every one of us is different but know this—there isn't one person on earth incapable of championing their life—regardless of their story!

I have found that living my *new* life with constant uncertainty of illness has given me the courage to make my life more interesting and meaningful. I did not practice these things; they became a part of my life after I accepted my illness and adjusted my attitude accordingly. When you embrace these simple principles, you learn to let go of anger and frustration, and you allow a greater capacity for happiness.

Don't look backward and don't live in the past. Find something to hope for, because without hope, you can lose the will to live. A hopeful patient remains positive, determined, better able to cope, and more likely to have more significant relationships-those things translate into a better quality of life. I believe that the loss of hope exacerbates your symptoms. You are not the same person anymore so put that behind you immediately. Learn to set *new* and appropriate goals based on your new level of ability, without focusing on the misery present.

Take active steps to manage anxiety and depression where they exist. Eat a stone-age diet and exercise where possible. Get your body in the best condition that *you* can before you say to yourself, "I have tried everything." Each of us has to make the decision to live, and sometimes that decision needs to be revisited. You cannot climb a mountain by telling yourself one time that you intend to do it, you have to adjust your lifestyle to accommodate a strong will to move on. We all have something to live for. Sometimes you just have to figure out what you are living for, and then go get it.

SELF-HYPNOSIS AND MEDITATION: LEARNING TO DETATCH FROM YOUR PAIN

I believe that education is the path to wellness, and my mission is to help make sense of chronic illness. The myriad symptoms I am faced with every minute of every day are endless, and for me, the pain never ends. Illness had rendered me mostly disabled at one point, so I beg this question: Where do we go from here? Like many of you reading this and likely suffering from these or other chronic illnesses, the challenges life presents for us are also endless.

We learn to live life by a different set of rules from those not suffering from chronic illness. We redefine our lives and are tasked with re-learning much of what we have already learned, we restructure our activities to accommodate our shortcomings, we become dependent on medications, on physical aids, and on other people, to do just enough to get by, we suffer from psychological disorders like depression and anxiety, as a result of living with our illnesses, we fail, fall short, and let people down. We learn to survive one bad habit after another.

Life with chronic illness can sometimes seem like a tragedy. But that is not where the story ends. Life can be what you make it, even with disease. And we do not have to be consumed by our symptoms—especially chronic pain. It took me many years to learn that I do not respond to pretty much any medication or treatment for my pain, and it also took me many years of educating myself to find something outside the box that did address my pain. For me, the road seemed longer than it had to be, but reading this book will shorten the road for you.

I felt as though I could say "I tried everything, and nothing works" which was true from a traditional sense. As I would spend many hours lying there trying to talk myself out of pain, I began to calm myself to a point of deep meditation, which became a place where I could focus on the pain so deeply, that I could detach myself from it, visually the same way you would distance yourself from harmful stimuli.

Breathing and meditation in the fibro equation. An overlooked benefit in the chronic illness game is meditation and controlled breathing. Part of reclaiming control over your body and reversing fibromyalgia is controlling your environment. You cannot control your entire environment, so you attempt to control what you can control. That is a difficult thing to do, especially when you live in a stress promoting environment as most of us do. The trick is to create the right kind of environment that puts you in control of your whole world long enough to reduce symptoms for just a little while. You isolate yourself and meditate. You calm yourself for half an hour by controlled breathing to bring you closer to homeostasis. Meditation is considered an art, which means you can become a master at it. Mastering meditation means mastering your breathing and this provides a degree of pain and symptom relief.

Just as most medications do not work for everyone, neither does hypnosis or meditation, and for me, it does not alleviate pain, it just allows me to draw my focus elsewhere, and detach from the pain. This has literally reduced my pain baseline and my pain threshold, and I am able to *live again*. This is not something I can teach and clearly I have not done a thorough job explaining it, but discover it for yourself through education about meditation and hypnosis and learn how to distance yourself from your pain.

FINDING HOPE IN HOPELESSNESS: MY STORY OF SURVIVAL

I have spent way too much of my time the last two decades in a horizontal position telling myself, I am in too much pain to get up. Chronic illness is often comorbid with depression, and I am not above this paradigm myself. I address my psychological shortcomings related to chronic pain using CBT, guided imagery, self-hypnosis, meditation, yoga, and positive psychology interventions. This multi-faceted approach covers all of the much needed variables that can lead to greater disability, and reinforces the most important modality of wellness-attitude.

Without maintaining a positive attitude throughout your illness, you are destined to fail, and you will never achieve wellness. This often means finding hope where there is none. How do you find hope when it seems so obvious that there is none to be found? By aligning all of these principles with your personal mission to get beyond your illness, and never looking back. You find the tools you need to get there, and you stop being the victim. My wellness approach delivers me to a state of health that is less than optimal, but I continue to remain hopeful. This translates into an improvement, as long as you are looking at your situation with the right perspective and attitude, as I do.

Illness has taken more from me than I can ever describe. I have faced numerous layers of loss. I am a completely different person today, versus who I was when I was well. Sometimes I cannot remember what it was like to view the world through healthy eyes and see myself whole again. But somehow I managed to achieve getting through college with a disabling illness. While growing my education and most other daily functions for that matter present great challenges for me, it has also shown me what it means to be strong when all I possess is weakness. It has shown me how to be brave when all I face is fear. It has taught me to be an example of what can be out of what is, and overall my health challenges have made me a better person as a result.

I understand what it means to be constantly ill, and I understand what it means to be in chronic pain every minute of every day, in every part of my body, but what I will never understand, is how I could ever let those circumstances stop me from being the most I can be with what I was given, or how I could ever let my illness stand in my way. I challenge myself every day to push beyond yesterday, and some days I lose that challenge. We fight anger and frustration constantly. Small losses like that are insignificant in the big picture of my goal of wellness. The idea that "you can do anything you set your mind to do" means everything to a sick person, and when you get your attitude wrapped around your hope-nothing will stand in your way. In the face of great adversity—*I have arrived.*

SLEEP

The lack of sleep can cripple even the healthiest of people. No one more than someone with FM can truly understand what poor sleep or sleep deprivation means. The very nature of our illness *chronic fatigue* is what throws our sleep systems out of whack. A typical day for us is to experience erratic patterns of fatigue followed by *episodes* of pure fatigue in its most debilitating form, causing us to nap at all different times of the day, when we are not acting like zombies, throwing off our sleep cycle.

We need to continue to work toward a *sleep schedule* that is as consistent as we can make it because our sleep is crucial. *Sleep latency* describes the time it takes a person to fall asleep. This period can seem like a no-brainer, but is actually more scientific than you think. Having the sleep environment perfect during sleep latency will allow you to fall asleep faster, which means: no TV, no radio, no reading, no computer, no distractions, just sleep. Going to bed and getting up around the same time everyday conditions us to form a habit which involves commitment at some level. That is why *sleep maintenance* is important, and describes undisturbed sleep. With FM, you have many things that can keep you up at night like pain, insomnia, and anxiety, etc. But you can also have issues that keep you from remaining asleep like: apnea, restless legs syndrome, insomnia, pain, medications, or bladder issues, etc. I can assign a whopping four times the pain and fatigue value on the days after I don't sleep well versus pre FM. Good sleep maintenance can lead to good *sleep architecture*, which fosters the right environment for regenerative sleep that heals and restores body functions, otherwise unable to be reached by someone with fibro.

Research about FM currently suggests some sort of low impact, moderate exercise as a balanced part of your recovery, which will improve and regulate your sleep patterns. At the end of the day maintaining an exercise curriculum will likely cause a lot of pain and fatigue but it can be good for the cardiovascular system, the muscles, your sleep, and your psychology. Conversely, the moment you *overdue* your exercise regime, you could cause a setback, so tread carefully. Remember pacing.

So many things work differently for so many sufferers that is why owning a program like this, starting with proper sleep, is your roadmap to getting your life back, or at least getting one step beyond disability. Activity is what we all fear and begin to move away from late in our illness because paying the price for overdoing it is an exaggerated understatement when you have FM. It is still unclear to researchers why we suffer our own body attacking itself after activity and not repairing itself during sleep. This phenomenon is known as *delayed fatigue*, or *post-exertional malaise*, and is the key hallmark symptom that keeps most of us unreliable and many of us disabled.

There are two types of sleep: rapid eye movement (REM) and non-rapid eye movement (NREM). Our mental recovery occurs in REM sleep and our physical recovery occurs during NREM sleep. There are four stages of NREM deep sleep and recovery depends on reaching all four levels (nih.gov).

During stage-four sleep, (delta sleep) the body releases the growth hormone *somatomedin C* which directs the repair of muscles. The *alpha EEG* anomaly explains fibro sleep issues by stopping stage-four sleep and lowering hormones. The other way to improve the release of GH is through exercising (nih. gov). Knowing what we know about FM, we are likely seriously deficient in GH since we are not sleeping well and not exercising enough either.

Appropriate sleep is a must while you are on the road to recovery. Poor sleep affects our mental capacity, our physical stamina, and most importantly, it affects our body's healing every day. I understand that 90 percent of us with FM do not ever reach the deep sleep cycle that fosters repairs during stage three and four sleep. The lack of quality sleep then becomes a perpetuating factor that affects other symptoms, not to mention unrelenting day time fatigue.

DELAYED FATIGUE

Delayed fatigue is the theory behind why we have symptom flare-ups for days after physical activity. Typical FM sufferers lack the stamina and strength to work on a *sustained* basis, largely in part due to delayed fatigue. Actually, for many of us, it is delayed flu-like everything. In FM there is an exaggerated and inappropriate response to physical activity of almost any kind, resulting in metabolic fatigue. This fatigue seems to be a response to a hormonal breakdown or inadequate response. It is thought that often thyroid or adrenal insufficiency is the culprit in FM, but since this is still misunderstood, I will not pretend to completely explain it.

It also seems clear that when you have FM, you have an insufficiency in adenosine triphosphate (ATP), or a mitochondrial dysfunction that contributes to delayed fatigue (nih.gov). Actually, it is much more than just delayed fatigue that you experience. Typically, you experience the myriad symptoms of FM during this *flare* and depending upon the individual, you may be totally wiped out.

While the rest of the world benefits from exercise and fitness, we tend to have opposite physical reactions and often the effect can seem counterproductive to our therapy or wellness. The bottom line is that twenty minutes of cardio can cause a week setback for some; making exercise feels like a no-no all the time. The key is finding what works within these parameters. tai chi and yoga are suggested to be two forms of low impact exercise that provide the needed physical benefit for FM. You have to experiment and find out what level of exercise works for you.

THE FUNCTIONAL CAPACITY EVALUATION

The functional capacity examination is a tool for doctors, insurance companies, and the court systems, etc., to determine your physical ability. It is used in disability litigation every day and has been used to determine whether or not FM is a valid disability. This exam was developed years ago for much different types of injuries or illnesses where more acute types of symptoms are present during this type of exam.

For example, when a person with a back injury exerts past their physical limits, they may have immediate pain or inability to continue the activity; resulting in an increase in their symptoms, and an obvious change in their condition. With FM, of course, we know there is not always an immediate worsening of symptoms that is obvious to those around us, hence the misunderstood illness. The FCE was likely simply carried over to be used with FM since nothing else existed, even though its validity may be questioned concerning FM.

This examination has been a tool used by private disability providers to determine whether or not you are capable of working, or if you are disabled; after all, it makes sense that they demand proof. It seems that this exam, more often than not, would disapprove individuals their right to benefits for years. This seems very unfortunate to me because the exam is completely invalid for FM. This is exactly the fundamental misunderstanding of delayed fatigue!

The problem with this exam is that it only takes a few hours and it will be scheduled on a random day that may or may not be a day that you may or may not be functioning well. The exam does not even take into account a typical work day. This exam does not take into account the delayed fatigue effect of not just FM, but many other disabilities and illnesses as well. No consideration is given to the fact that FM symptoms wax and wane from one minute to the next, so crawling or climbing stairs at 10:00

a.m. on Monday may not be as difficult as it is at 3:00 p.m. on Wednesday—day after day, week after week. No one comes and examines you the next day, or for that matter over the course of the next week to see how you are progressively impacted by *post-exertion delayed flare-ups*, which for most of us are cumulative. All of this speaks to the physical shortcomings that plague FM sufferers but consideration should be given to the cognitive ones as well. This drastically underestimates the true aspect of the illness and further the disability it poses on your everyday life. The other thing to consider with regard to post-exertion fatigue is that both the typical duration and severity of the cycle or flare are dramatically exaggerated the longer the activity is performed; again not taken into account during the FCE.

Having FM does not always mean you cannot walk or bend over and touch your toes or read an eye chart. It is this exact kind of exam that discredits an individual of having a valid, disabling illness. With the exception of a very few disabilities that exist, almost anyone who suffers from a disability can successfully pass a FCE exam, for the most part. If you catch a FM sufferer on a good day, they can *function*! If you catch them on a bad day; you will have to help them out of bed just like any other well deserving disabled person. This is not to say that the exam itself is faulty, it's just not valid for FM, *like most other standardized testing procedures.*

I think it is difficult deciding who is disabled and who is not today. After all, there is overwhelming controversy surrounding the topic, and I do not think anyone has a sound answer right now. What is logical and important to me in deciding who is disabled may boil down to a number of things. It starts with objectivity in the patient's character. If someone is lying or malingering it will be apparent soon enough. If someone is chasing a cure and taking the necessary steps to help themselves get well, at significant personal sacrifice, they are likely being honest, even when the system may make you feel like you have to sometimes do whatever it takes to make those in power believe you. Having a history of supporting medical documentation will help most people, with some exceptions—it may not help to have the doctor's notes from those doctors who did not believe you or who sent you away or wrote that you were a hypochondriac in your file! These kinds of notes may make you look like a neurotic patient, despite the growing popularity of FM.

So overall the opinion of the medical profession matters forever so keep that in mind when you interact with them. And finally your records of your history with the illness will help make sense of your story. It is not easy to sift through 20 years of garbled notes from an FM patient, but as you go-document-and you will not regret that you did. What you did, how you felt, what medications you took, etc. This history overall can be passed on as needed and can serve as your walking wellness plan and will help you as you make your way. Finally, we just need more time to research more answers on FM to know where to go from here.

SHOULD I TELL MY EMPLOYER ABOUT MY FIBROMYALGIA?

There are more and more people each year diagnosed with and learning to live with fibromyalgia. This means there are more and more people in the work force with fibro. The Americans with Disabilities Act provides guidelines for *accommodations* that *some* employers are supposed to make for those working with disabilities.

This is not to say that just because you have fibro, you are automatically disabled from work, or need accommodation, but some people will. So the question is raised, do I tell my employer I have fibro? To me this is not a simple yes or no answer. My answer is *it depends*, because many employers will make only very slight accommodations for disabilities *when* required by law to do so, and most employers will not say it, but do not have the room for employees with limitations or special needs; especially those employees needing extra breaks, longer lunches, and more sick days off.

So then should I *not* tell my employer? Again, it is not a simple yes or no answer. If you have no choice but to work, and your disability or limitations get in the way of your job, you may have to inform your employer because sooner or later you will not be able to hide your shortcomings, and if you miss extra work due to fibro, you will run out of valid excuses fast.

This becomes a very complex situation. As an employee, you should know your rights, but as an employee with physical or mental job limitations, it becomes essential that you know what you can and cannot do, what you should and should not do, and what your employer can and cannot do to you. Knowing your rights means knowing what you can *get away with* as a person with a disability, and still keep your job.

These laws are specific to each state in most cases, minus a few laws that are federally imposed. If you are in need of special or *reasonable accommodations* to perform your job on a *sustained* basis, you may need to approach someone at work to request the special accommodation such as a special chair, an ergonomic keyboard, a work area near a bathroom, adjusted lights above you, a flexible schedule, or part time status, etc.

Besides the potential embarrassment of informing your boss that you have fibro, your whole department may soon know that something is going on, and to avoid coworkers from becoming angry at you for slacking off, taking extra breaks, or missing too much work. You may have to figure out a way to break the news to everyone working near you. Maybe you can get away with only informing your human resources department, who can make accommodations for you without the rest of the staff knowing why. But at some point, your coworkers may find out one way or another, assuming your work is impacted.

If you work for a small employer, like more than half the country does, you may have to be much more open about your limitations or special needs. This is where it really depends on your relationship with your boss. If your boss likes you, values your contribution to the organization, and literally has the ability to make accommodations, he likely will.

The problem with small employers is that there may not be money in the budget to make special accommodations like purchasing expensive ergonomic office equipment, or allowing you to work flextime when you don't feel well enough to come to work. If you work for a company that has five or six employees for example, your contribution is likely critical, which may translate into your employer *not* being able to work around your health condition—whether they want to or not.

All employers do not have to make special accommodations for disabled employees. For example, according to Title I of the ADA ACT, (below) protection fall on employers with fifteen or more employees. Further, the term *undue hardship* in the ADA ACT means that if the accommodation costs too much money, employers do not have to make it. Plus you would need a medical status that states you are disabled, likely from a physician or judge to be legitimate.

> ADA Title I: Employment (ada.gov)
> Title I requires employers with 15 or more employees to provide qualified individuals with disabilities an equal opportunity to benefit from the full range of employment-related opportunities available to others. For example, it prohibits discrimination in recruitment, hiring, promotions, training, pay, social activities, and other privileges of employment. It restricts questions that can be asked about an applicant's disability before a job offer is made, and it requires that employers make reasonable accommodation to the known physical or mental limitations of otherwise qualified individuals with disabilities, unless it results

in undue hardship. Religious entities with 15 or more employees are covered under title I.

So, the choice to inform your employer that you have a disability is yours and comes down to a number of factors. Think your situation through, and know your rights and all the laws that may apply to your situation.

EXERCISE AND FIBROMYALGIA

Exercise is a large component in the fibro equation as well as general wellness and I place a lot of emphasis on diet and exercise reversing fibromyalgia. Exercise plays an obvious role in promoting wellness. How exercise translates into the puzzle piece that will tip the pain scale toward relief is this: When blood flow and oxygen are increased around your nerves (those nerves that are causing increased pain signals from the brain), they are allowed to relax. This relaxation of nerve sensors promotes a reduction in pain. Exercise promotes re-conditioning and strengthens every part of the body as well as releases endorphins, the feel good hormone that reduces pain naturally, which is *exercise analgesia.*

Over the past several years there has been a debate about exercise and fibromyalgia—does it provide a benefit or does it just promote post exertional malaise? I have interviewed a number of physicians and medical experts who all have varying opinions, but most of whom feel that there are more benefits overall to exercise; even though I have met a handful who were dead set against exercise with fibro.

I have also interviewed a number of fibro patients, the majority of who feel that exercise provides no benefit whatsoever and in fact causes more pain and fatigue overall, adding to their feeling of general malaise. This debate centers on post-exertional malaise and the deconditioning phenomenon. Deconditioning, or disuse atrophy, is the weakening, fatiguing, and potential damaging of muscles, joints, and surrounding tissues as a result of being sedentary. The longer you remain sedentary, the more likely you will experience pain and fatigue when you do begin to exert yourself by exercising. Deconditioning is not specific to fibro of course, but since there are such a large number of individuals suffering from fibro, by default, there are also a large number of fibro patients experiencing deconditioning.

It is a fact that exercising releases endorphins, the feel good hormone, which promotes a decrease in pain and fatigue. Endorphins also act to reduce stress and anxiety, improve sleep, strengthen your heart, lower blood pressure, improve muscle strength, helps build bones, and reduce fat. The release of endorphins also contributes to a reduction in depression, which can lower pain and fatigue symptoms. Plus you stand to benefit from exercise psychologically by improving your self-esteem, anxiety, and depression—all from the release of endorphins. And finally, endorphins act as pain relievers and sedatives, thereby reducing pain overall.

With fibro, we have pain without damage or injury, and some would argue that fibro pain is in the head versus the body, making it psychological or neurological. I argue that exercise is another example that proves fibro is a physical, biological illness versus a psychological one. In fibro there is a marked increase in opioid receptors in the periphery and spinal cord, and a decreased amount of receptors in the brain. This makes you less sensitive to opioids, and more sensitive to pain, especially from exertion. Plus, fibro patient's often are found to have an increase of endogenous opioids making you sensitive to opioids and hypersensitive to pain in general.

There is also a suggested difference in activation of the pain-sensitive areas of the brain, which means there is an increase regional brain blood flow as discovered by fMRI. This means that when there is an increased blood flow to specific areas of the brain, that there is an increased activity in that region. The insula is the area of the brain that is sensitive or on high suggesting an increase in pain signals. This results in abnormal pain processing. The fMRI also has been used to identify overactivity in the CNS.

Exercise increases energy and stimulates tired tissues, aids in depression symptoms, promotes healthier, more restorative sleep, promotes memory, concentration and overall cognition, and it reduces the likelihood of frequent mood swings. Exercise can help many of our fibro symptoms. The best way to nourish the nerves that cause pain is through movement. Movement of the body moves the nerves which pump blood and oxygen to that nerve, relaxing it, and reducing inflammation and pain. Exercise allows the nerve sensors to calm down, making the brain *understand* what is happening so it does not over react. This is part of reversing fibromyalgia through education and understanding pain.

It is no secret that fitness is important regardless of who you are. The end result of most chronic illnesses is some level of deconditioning from the lack of movement. The longer you go without steady activity, stretching, exercise, etc., the more susceptible you will be to comorbidity, among other things, like weight gain, pneumonia, blood clots, increased pain, and fatigue. Exercise helps to control pain levels and tolerance which leads to increased recovery times and proper immune system function- which is one of the ingredients to general wellness. If you simply choose to control your pain with opioids and omit fitness, consider this: opioids cause changes in the central nervous system which promotes wind-up pain and hyperalgesia that exacerbate pain.

Exercising with a chronic illness like fibromyalgia can be difficult and painful. It can seem as though it is not helping and only causes more pain and fatigue. The reality is that the wheels turn very slow with fibro and so will results from exercise. You cannot expect results similar to those who do not suffer from chronic illness. Everything becomes a greater challenge when you are chronically ill, and exercise is no exception. What will truly work for most if not all people is starting low and going slow.

Join a fitness center because it will commit you to something. It will promote the social aspect of your life that is likely reduced anyway. Make plans to just decide to go to the gym-this is a good start. If you physically make it to the gym you are likely to stay. If you stay you are likely to walk around and find something that seems like you could do it without too much regret. And once you get started, you will go until you are tired and you slowly increase what you do.

Make plans to exercise with others because it will put you on the hook to stand by your commitment. Try to go two to three times a week, and maybe don't establish which days those will be yet-play it by ear and go when you have peak energy. Don't wait to go when you are not in pain because you will never go. The whole idea is to exercise to reduce symptoms-which does work. It may seem like it does not work for weeks, but you need to stick with some kind of steady commitment, and the energy will come as the pain reduces.

I get it that this may sound like a challenge you are not up for, *but* I promise that you will continue to de-condition and essentially go down-hill if you neglect this one aspect of your wellness plan. In just two years, you can go from healthy and vibrant to nearly bedridden and miserable. Join a gym. Decide to go. Set goals. Keep commitments. Stick with it. Start low-go slow.

When you are afflicted with fibro, lupus, arthritis, or MS, etc., you may already be on your way to becoming physically deconditioned. Deconditioning presents numerous problems, but can essentially be reversed with a simple fitness plan. It is suggested that you discuss exercising with your physician, and most physicians will tell you to exercise, even with chronic illness. Exercise essentially becomes a powerful treatment modality for otherwise difficult to treat illnesses.

Muscles are required to be used in order to continue working properly. But our cardiovascular system needs to be exercised as well so that complications involving the heart, lungs, and vascular system, etc., do not occur or exacerbate. Our goal as a person with a chronic illness is not that different than a physically healthy individual, which is to maintain health through the maintaining of muscle integrity and circulation. Joints rely on muscle integrity and tone and the calcification of bones—the result of continued movement. Again, when you don't use it, you actually do lose it.

With an illness like fibro, often you face post-exertional malaise and fatigue, which subsequently can increase when you exercise. A large majority of those with chronic illnesses are capable of some form of exercise. When done correctly, exercise benefits every part of the body. Exercise builds and maintains muscle integrity and tone, supports and stabilizes joints, reduces fatigue, and increases movement.

It is suggested that you do not exercise while in the middle of a severe flare as it may exacerbate pain or fatigue and actually be dangerous. Being overly achy and fatigued may be the right time to pass on exercising. Personally, I train four to five days a week as rigorously as possible and I will take two days off a week for recovery. So this program is not that different from a healthy person. Yes it will be harder for you with fibro and yes you will have more pain and fatigue than a healthy person.

The exceptions are that I work out with less weight, less intensity, and shorter duration. But I am seeing differences in my general pain and fatigue levels. Additionally, while my body weight is reducing, I am seeing some muscle definition breaking through. So stopping or reducing your exercise because you are in a flare is up to you. Considering that you may always be in pain and always be exhausted how does one exercise in this condition? You just do it. You dig deep and get it done and I guarantee you will feel better in the long run.

Is an injury while exercising more likely with fibro? It is also suggested that intense exercising while deconditioned, or after time off for a flare may cause injuries or just extra pain. In this case, cardio like biking or elliptical are okay for times like these. In fact when I began exercising after a long period away from it, I did cardio only for about two months to prepare my body for more rigorous workouts in the future. Plus, my re-entry into the fitness arena was a slow-go since my pain and fatigue were always high and my recovery was very slow. This way, I only had to deal with minor recovery versus a full out body-builder-type recovery.

This is all objective, physiological evidence that those with fibro have a higher sensitivity to pain. The source of these abnormal processes is still unknown for the most part, but it is suspected that abnormal brain processing is involved. So what does this all mean in the grand scheme of exercising and fibro? Essentially, almost everyone needs to stay moving to avoid deconditioning. The lack of moving and deconditioning itself exacerbate pain and fatigue. So those with fibro need to find the right balance with an exercise regimen. Unless your knowledge about physiology is broad, you may work out for months and never figure out exactly what works with your body type/illness.

The answer may be to find an exercise physiologist to help you determine the correct exercise program that reduces pain versus increase pain. An exercise physiologist can tailor a plan to suit your particular level of pain and/or deconditioning. They specialize in creating an exercise curriculum for those with illnesses and injuries. If wellness is your goal, then you need to participate in some kind of exercise—no question. I think it goes without saying that exercise is a fundamental part of a healthy lifestyle with very few exceptions.

SUMMARY OF EXERCISING WITH FIBRO

At the end of the day, exercise provides numerous health benefits, even for those suffering from fibromyalgia. In general, it may be best to participate in aerobic conditioning when you have a chronic illness like fibro at least to start. This type of exercise is low impact and may be all you are capable of, and will likely not exacerbate your symptoms as much as isometric strength training. Your exercise tolerance will increase, even with chronic illness. Don't over-do it. You need to know your body and your specific pattern of symptoms to know how much is too much or when the timing is wrong to exercise. If you go into exercising too hard or too fast you will be in pain and be likely to quit altogether as a result. Expect some pain during and after exercise with fibro. If you are having an inflamed joint issue, don't work out that area because you will likely exacerbate it. You have to work within your limitations, but don't give up when the going gets tough. My advice is to participate in as aggressive of a routine as you can, and settle for aerobic exercise or cardio when necessary because there are invisible results like reducing the risk of heart disease and depression, etc. Remember, exercising is a coping strategy to combat illness. Exercise is great medicine. And nothing feels as good as fit looks.

NUTRITION AND FIBROMYALGIA

Nutrition, like exercise, also plays an obvious role in promoting wellness. How nutrition translates into the puzzle piece that will tip the pain scale toward relief is this: When you supply the body with the wrong food you create a disease promoting internal environment. When you eat processed foods, you starve your body of nutrition. When you eat sugary foods, you promote inflammation and destructive free radicals. These both translate into fatigue producing effects that exacerbate your symptoms. Fatigue causes you to do less because it is too hard to do more. It changes your attitude to become negative and it promotes deconditioning, which is a certain recipe for further disease and greater disability.

You are what you eat, and some of us are extra-large servings of chocolate cake! No diet has been proven to influence FM one way or another, at least officially. Since there are so many factors that have to be looked at in the FM patient, it is difficult to know what foods are problems. Today, practically everything in the grocery store can have a negative effect on our myriad symptoms, which makes our diet become a difficult program in our recovery especially since we spend so much time consumed by it physically, and the balance of our time consumed by it emotionally.

Research has suggested that imbalances in nutrition can lead to new symptoms, exacerbate your current symptoms, and lead to chronic conditions. Nutrition is the most critical component to your wellness approach long-term. Healthy nutritional choices are the first step to correcting your deficiencies. When you are as healthy as you can get yourself, you are essentially doing everything you can to allow your physician to help you. He will be able to assess a baseline for you and this will save critical time trying to figure out which directions to go in as you recover, as well as determine which medications are working sooner. If you are a non-compliant patient who has a number of self-management issues, such as overeating, obesity, food allergies, carb addictions, a higher degree of alcohol and caffeine consumption, etc., this will only add to the severity of your symptoms and to the duration of your recovery.

What we have to do is open a new functional growing chapter in our lives and label it nutrition for wellness. This chapter will play a significant role in your battle against FM and serve as a baseline for your maintenance *after* you have moved on to a maintenance stage of the illness. There is nothing more obvious to Americans than the notion that *good nutrition fosters good health* as a general rule. We see it every day in every form of marketing at home, work, school, and in stores. Wouldn't it be great if we became a nation that lived by nutritional labels on food cartons?

There is a rule we have to live by. Most of us have special or delicate dietary considerations to deal with *now* that we have FM. Many foods do not agree with FM and the many dysfunctions caused by the illness. That is why our diets are more critical than those without FM. This is a difficult, time consuming, and often constantly fluctuating task to find agreeable foods and moreover the right quantities. Our dietary needs change often creating yet another perpetuating factor-if you do not stoke the fire with the right fuel the fire goes out. This is where the whole topic of ATP and mitochondria and energy production comes into play.

From birth, we are consumed by consumption. Our first real love is food, and the comfort it provides us as babies. The fact is that for many people, we never outgrow that love for food and specifically comfort foods, which come in the form of bad, terrible, and worse. A dietitian would tell a normal, healthy person to avoid most processed foods just for good measure. FM sufferers have it twice as bad for so many reasons that our bodies do not digest, process, and eliminate foods the same as healthy individuals. And if you have viruses or bacteria as possible underlying causes, you are likely vitamin and mineral deficient. Then consider hormonal and glandular dysfunction and you are a complete mess. It can take a long time to determine what your body's response levels are, and you will come to realize that a solid diet will benefit you for long-term maintenance of your FM.

The critical role of protein with fibro. Protein helps your body recover after exercising. The body has an increased need for protein as a fuel to repair muscles after exercising—especially after intense or long duration activity. Protein is the third source of fuel used for energy—carbs being first, and fats being second. Studies have shown that the typical US diet exceeds the US RDA for protein. Note: Energy comes first from carbs, which comes from blood sugars first, then muscle glycogen, then fat begins to burn for energy, finally, protein becomes a fuel source.

Exercising requires more energy and therefore an increase of protein is needed. There currently exists an intense debate about the physiological effects of protein ingestion before, during, and after exercise, as well as carb needs related to exercise. I tend to agree with one school of thought that the protein needs of the active person are higher than the sedentary person.

The US RDA does not suggest that athletes or those who exercise intensely need an increased amount of protein, however, many scientists would disagree. So who is lacking protein? Some populations may lack protein in their diet, and therefore need to increase protein through diet or supplementation. Low consuming people, women, those trying to lose weight, the elderly, the *ill*, and *deconditioned individuals*-may all need more protein intake.

When does protein get used as a fuel? Again, protein is the body's third choice for fuel, after carbs and fats. As you exercise, you deplete your carb stores, which initially fuel exercise. At this point, the goal for some people is to burn fat and lose weight, or for others it is to build muscle. Amino acids can begin to be broken down and used for fuel after the carbs are depleted, but the typical contribution by protein to exercising is about five percent. Try to eat 8–12 grams of protein within an hour after exercising and a total of 60 grams per day on average.

So when do you decide to take protein supplementation or amino acid supplements? Experts suggest that an athlete should maintain 10–15 percent of their daily energy intake from protein. This is also the popular theory. This means that you can likely get your protein needs through diet alone. I think the debate will continue as to whether or not *extra* protein provides benefits for exercise.

Are protein supplements superior to food proteins? No. It is proven that optimal protein needs can be met through diet alone, and supplements can vary considerably. For muscle growth, loading up on essential amino acids is better than non-essential amino acids (if you plan to load up), and can be found in fish, most all meats, eggs, most diary, peanut butter, soy, tofu, and beans. Eating plant-based proteins (cheese or nuts or veggies etc.) with animal-based proteins (meats or fish etc.) is optimal. If you eat enough plant based proteins, like beans, lentils, grains, and veggies you can avoid the animal based proteins, which are inferior for reasons like cholesterol and disease.

What is the right protein amount? Overloading on protein beyond the recommended quantities for *you*, is likely not any more beneficial than taking the suggested amount. Amino acids are suggested to supply a two-hour stimulation to muscle tissue. This suggests that eating numerous small doses of proteins versus one large dose of protein may be just as beneficial.

Can you consume too much protein? Some research suggests that you can. Too much protein may overtax the kidneys. The issue becomes that if you mega-dose protein, you still have to synthesize it or break it down into amino acids, which produces the by-product nitrogen (a toxin) that has to be removed by the kidneys. This can lead to dehydration if you don't take in enough water, which is usually not an issue for those who exercise regularly, but may be an issue for those with fibro. The other issue is that excess protein will be converted to fat and stored.

What about exercise recovery? When you exercise vigorously you increase protein synthesis and breakdown in your muscles for up to a day after your workout. The reason it is suggested that you consume a protein meal or shake after a workout is that if you don't reintroduce protein to your recovering muscles, protein breakdown will exceed protein synthesis, which can result in muscle loss versus gain. This step needs to be avoided with chronic illnesses. While carbs after exercise are needed to replenish muscle glycogen stores that were depleted early in exercising, protein's role is to repair and synthesize new protein for recovery. After exercising, you may only need eight to 12 grams of protein to make this happen, and again, consume the protein within an hour after exercising.

I think like most things out there today, the marketing around performance products exceeds the actual scientific evidence in the lab. Meaning companies hype their products beyond scientific expectations. But the psychology controls the biology, so if you *think it,* it will be done, to some degree. So living your life with a structured diet and some extra hope in there that your efforts will be amplified by doing certain things, like consuming extra proteins, is certainly worth a shot. Note: Stay hydrated constantly, before, during, and after exercising, and make sure you replace fluids lost from sweat.

Burning fat with chronic illness. Exercising is different for different types of people, like

(a) those who want to gain muscle size
(b) those who want to shred up and get down to a low body fat percentage
(c) those who want to lose weight, or even

(d) those who suffer from injury or illness and just need conditioning. Depending on your needs or expectations, your workout will be different than other peoples are

As a general rule, your body burns either fat or carbohydrates depending on what you physically do in the gym. You are always burning fat no matter what you are doing, in small doses, but losing weight amounts to either reducing the amount of calories you consume or increasing the amount of calories you burn. Your body also burns carbs all the time, until they are gone, at which time your body will burn fats. So just sitting in a chair you are burning calories, roughly 60 percent from fat and 40 percent from carbs; amounting to around one to two calories burning a minute on average, not during workouts. With age, we lose muscle mass and our metabolism slows down, making it harder to achieve goals in the gym and weight loss the older we get. This goes double for chronic illness.

As you begin to exercise, your body will use the carbs you have stored and the ratio becomes roughly 70 percent carbs and 30 percent fat. Carbs can deplete quick though since you have limited stores of them in the body and the next fuel source is fats. When this happens, the ratio again switches to something like 60 percent fat and 40 percent carb fuel usage. The better condition you are in, the more efficiently your body will make those metabolic transitions, keeping you fit. Remember that with fibro, it is suggested that we often have metabolic dysfunctions that may inhibit our metabolism from working efficiently.

The simple principle is that you need to burn as many calories as you consume or you will gain weight. If you burn slightly more calories than you consume, you will lose weight. It all starts with diet. One or two days a week is not enough cardio if your goal is to lose weight. If you are at a desirable, healthy weight, you can do less cardio. If you have fibro this will seem like an insurmountable task but a necessary one. So exercising burns calories, but it doesn't necessarily promote weight loss. How the calories are burned matter more than what the fuel source was that burned those calories-whether it was fats or carbs. Diet becomes the critical factor in calorie burning.

Losing weight from exercising. If you want to lose fat you will want to exercise with a higher intensity like running, elliptical, or stair climber versus walking or yoga. Sometimes burning extra fat from exercising does not result in weight loss. This end result depends on the total number of calories burned from fat and carbs; so if you exercise at a slower rate, like walking or light yoga etc., you will have to do it longer. Doing cardio for a short time, say ten minutes, even intensely will not burn much fat as if you were to lower your intensity and increase your duration. The reason why is that after you have been doing cardio for 15 minutes or so, your body will stop burning carbs and convert to burning fats, translating into reducing your weight.

If you were to sit down and read a book for 20 minutes, you are burning roughly 40 calories, of which the percentage would be 60 percent fat and 40 percent carbs, which translates into 24 of those calories you burned will have come from fat. If you were to walk for 20 minutes, you are burning roughly 100 calories; percentage is 65 percent fat, 35 percent carbs, which will burn 65 calories from fat stores. And finally if you were to run, do elliptical, or a stair climber for 20 minutes, you are burning around 250 calories. This time the percentage of fat burned reduces to 40 percent and the calories burned from fat are around 100. So you burn more calories doing this activity, even though not all come from fat-your body begins to burn quick energy carbs. Once the body becomes sustained it will switch back and start burning fat again. So short workout equals less burned fat. Long workout equals more burned fat. Intense workout equals more burned carbs than fats, but still more calories total.

Can you burn fat just on your stomach? Not really. Science has shown that *spot reducing* of fat does not really work; you have to burn fat everywhere. Interval training is best for chronic illness next to cardio. If you work out with the same type of exercises every week, you will increase muscle memory and definition, but using interval training or circuit training, changing it up, *shocks* the system, the muscles, and the metabolism, resulting in a greater reduction of fat burning or calorie burning.

Too much fat, what to do? Some experts suggest that if you are overweight you may want to weight train two to three times a week, with a focus on one or two muscle groups. Other experts suggest that focusing on working out the whole body versus one or two muscle groups is the more optimum choice for weight loss. I think it depends on *you*. My program consists of weight training three to four days a week, cardio three to four days a week, and not even looking junk foods in the eyes.

Are sit-ups or abdominal workouts the answer to bust the stomach flab? Not really. While abdominal exercises will contribute to your overall fitness fame and they are the only way to get sculpted abs, if your diet is not solid, you are spinning your wheels. In other words, if you don't eat right, you can do hundreds of sit-ups a day and you will never bust your gut. Fat is 80 percent diet and 20 percent exercise.

So how is fat burned? The simple explanation is that if you use more energy than you consume, you will lose weight, as a rule, and depending on your genetics, this may be easier for some people. But don't get too hung up on the genetics thing, we can all lose weight. The body will burn carbs first, and fats next for fuel, and in some cases proteins are converted to glucose and used as fuel, usually in emergencies. This happens regardless of what activities you do. Burning fat is the body using your own tissue to fuel your activities. Carbs burn quick and first, and fats burns slow and later. All people benefit from the after effects of exercise where an increased metabolism stays *energized* for a time after you are done exercising; some more than others. Again, don't get hung up if you think your metabolism is *one of the slow ones* because it just means it takes a bit longer.

The body wants to burn glucose (usually from carbs) first, when the demand for fuel arises during exercise. Depending on your diet, your workout will use up what glucose stores you have available immediately, and then turn to fat stores for energy (but not right away). If you eat a lot of carbs, your body may never reach for the fat stores for fuel unless you work out like crazy, because it will grab for the readily available carbs for fuel. So after the glucose is all burned up from your blood and muscles, (your blood sugar drops) it begins to eat away your fat.

Does weight training burn fat? Yes weight training can burn extra fat. Just having more muscle than fat is suggested to burn more fat even at rest—but the difference is arguable either way. A blend of weight training and cardio is best, especially for weight loss but depends with chronic illness of course.

So why do cardio if weight training burns fat? Weight training provides benefits like more strength, stronger bones and joints, and better conditioning overall, whereas cardio provides benefits to the heart, lungs, blood pressure, and arteries etc., which are things weight training benefit much less. And, weight training only burns roughly half the calories that cardio does. With fibro we need to do both to reverse our illness.

What time of the day is the best time to burn fat? After a meal is best; first thing in the morning does not benefit some people. So what is the *right* diet? Taking supplements or diet pills or foods that speed up metabolism are not the answer. Fitness doesn't come in a pill or a *diet*, it comes with eating less calories than you burn off, or burning off more calories than you eat. It means eating more of the right kinds of foods like whole foods, veggies, and unprocessed foods, and less of the SAD, or standard American diet foods like fast foods, soda, and junk foods. Eat when you are hungry, not when you are bored, and don't use food as a reward or a comfort.

Should I stretch before or after exercising or both? Stretching before exercising (static stretching) is likely to not help avoid injuries, prevent post-exertional soreness, or muscle pain, and improve your workout; a pre-warm up may be better than a pre-stretch. Static stretching may actually cause muscles to tighten if done just before exercising. Stretching after exercising may be more beneficial to reduce post-exertional muscle pain and increase range of motion. A warm-up before exercising increases blood flow to the muscles, promoting muscle use. Even stretching at the end of the day is better than before exercising. Don't bounce stretch or ballistic stretch because it may promote injury. So, regarding burning fat, it starts with a good diet, and ends with a fitness lifestyle; change it up often, shock your system, and save time for cardio.

You can read numerous research based articles on FM and nutrition and you will likely find one common element which would be to avoid processed foods in general. A diet absent of processed foods, simple sugars, and basic junk food will serve you well as you fill your FM toolbox with weapons to defend yourself. It is not enough to say *avoid certain foods*; you have to be able to do it. There is so much more to getting your diet right but that is a solid starting point. Additionally, there may be a stigma that exists that diets are hard to follow, harder to stick to, and nearly impossible to maintain after desired results are achieved!

If this were true, and you are like me, you need a list of *go* and *no go* foods to live by. So without getting technical and speaking to the cellular level, there are a number of foods that you should avoid and those that you should include in your diet to eliminate any extra fat and perpetuating factors to your FM. Some foods do not perpetuate or exacerbate your symptoms, but they will make you fat since you move less now than you used to. Plus you need to figure out for yourself what foods are problems for you on your own since everyone is so different. The list I have comprised below, mostly foods high on the glycemic index, will most likely just aggravate you so let's just call it *food for thought*. (Don't feel stupid for not knowing this stuff; we can play dumb together).

I also want to plant the seed about nutrition as it existed more than one hundred years ago. There were almost zero processed foods and almost zero nutrition based illnesses. Illnesses such as adult diabetes, hypoglycemia, obesity, and certain cancers existed in a fraction of the numbers that exist today. And thinking globally about your diet may help too. Did you know that while in the US, fruit is at the top of healthy categories, but is hardly touched in China! Neither is cheese. When you compare our morbidity tables to those of other countries, we rate low on the healthy scale. Plus, in 1900, the average person consumed five pounds of sugar per year; today, the average person consumes 150 pounds of sugar per year. Sugar promotes disease.

I always suggest to people with fibro to eat a very specific diet such as whole foods—why whole foods, because it will be in its most natural form, unadulterated and untreated. Eat raw foods—why raw foods, again, because these foods will be natural, unadulterated, and untreated and because it will contain live probiotics and enzymes that are eliminated through cooking and processing. These foods will not have anything artificial added, especially through processing. Eat organic foods where possible-why organic foods, because these foods will contain a wider assortment of vitamin and minerals found in nature, but often not found in the foods we eat; if it comes from a plant eat it. Eat cultured dairy versus uncultured dairy for their probiotics. Cook foods yourself so you know what is in them. Eat slow, chew food completely. *Eat when you are hungry not when you are bored*. And since there are gaps in any diet, supplementation is not a bad idea either *if necessary* (find out from your physician). If you only take three supplements, make them: a raw whole foods multivitamin, a raw probiotic, and a concentrated Omega 3.

Do eat: 4–6 meals a day under 300 calories where possible high protein and low carbs. We are in an energy crisis and our slower metabolism does not help. By eating more than the traditional three meals a day, we train our metabolism to operate more often, which benefits us in absorption, digestion, and caloric use, increasing our energy production. This may not work for everyone since the result could be an overtaxed digestive system. Add foods that boost metabolism like almonds, apples, beans, broccoli, cinnamon, curry, grapefruit, green tea, jalapenos, oatmeal, silk, spinach, and turkey. Adding high protein foods to each meal will benefit the overall quality of your diet like raw veggies, select fruits like apples, salad dressings made from olive oil, coconut oil, vinegar, fibers, and select nuts. Reduce fat intake and exercise. Adding high protein foods to each meal will benefit the overall quality of your diet.

Drinking as much water as you possibly can means you will remain hydrated, it aids in detoxifying which is critical when you are riddled with viruses or bacteria, and water fills up space in your stomach making you eat less-so does fiber. Remaining hydrated keeps your metabolism operating efficiently. Dehydration increases fatigue overall. More water needs to be consumed during high stress periods or if you exercise. If you have the typical frequent urinary issues with FM, then you may have more trips to the bathroom, but you will be cleansing your body in the process. Substitute water for soda and fruit juice where possible.

Tomatoes and Zucchini's are great fruit choices. Romaine lettuce or any greens really, wild or organic berries, avocados, figs, and pomegranates. Berries do not raise your blood sugar to dangerous levels like many fruits can, and helps regulates mechanisms and provides lots of fiber, vitamins and minerals, and phytochemicals that aid against disease. Avocados are an excellent source of raw fat which is needed in healing and natural health processes. They are high in vitamins and minerals, and the fatty acids found within aid in energy production.

Figs have more minerals than most other fruits and figs are high in potassium, calcium, and iron. Pomegranates are the number one source for protection against free radical damage and disease and they also have the highest concentration of antioxidants of all fruits. Apples are high in fiber, vitamins, minerals, and antioxidants. If you must eat fruit, eat the sugary ones every other day.

Sweet potatoes are loaded with carotenoids, vitamin C, potassium, and fiber. 100 percent whole grain bread contains many times over the amount of vitamins and minerals versus white bread. Broccoli has high levels of carotenoids, folic acid, and vitamins C. Watermelon is an excellent source of carotenoids and vitamin C. Beans are low in fat, inexpensive, high in protein, and are loaded with iron, folic acid, and fiber. Cantaloupe includes high volumes of vitamin C and A in one little slice. Spinach and Kale provide calcium, fiber, carotenoids, and vitamin C. Oatmeal provides soluble fiber that helps lower *bad* cholesterol. One percent milk is an excellent source of protein, with almost no fat and cholesterol. Eat grains like bulger, quinoa, amaranth, couscous, and millet. Eat fermented foods for their probiotic benefit. Eat pasture raised chicken and eggs. Keep in mind when you have FM you have more than desirable levels of harmful free radicals and need more antioxidants.

Don't eat: Fruits are good for you, but in unique cases or cases where weight loss is desired here are some fruits that you may want to avoid: oranges, grapefruits, bananas, persimmons, raisins, and green grapes. Red and green grapes are full of sugar and have almost no nutrition. And of course don't forget to avoid the fruit juice, since it is almost the same as drinking soda, sugar wise. Fruit juice and cocktail all have lots of sugars added, and sometimes corn syrup. There is more sugar in a glass of fruit juice than a Snickers bar, has no fiber in it and lots of preservatives. No soda, coffee, candy, baked goods, processed foods, white bread, breadsticks, fast food, dairy and if you want to be extreme, artificial sweeteners.

Dried fruit is similarly bad since it is loaded up with sugars. When you dry out the fruit, you eliminate the water, but almost all the sugar stays in the fruit. Popcorn is considered a healthy alternative to chips or maybe Pop Tarts, but the sugar values are the same, which makes this one fall off the list too. It is however, a teeny bit better than a 3 Musketeers, so indulge if you want. Baked beans have as much sugar in the syrup as a soda; while there remains a benefit of fiber, protein, and other nutrients. Choosing red kidney beans as an alternative because they are loaded with protein and fiber is better. Black beans are good too.

Fat free usually means it is the only thing of value, and is likely full of sugar and chemicals. Reduced fat usually means increased carbs. Foods on the *low fat* list are usually not on the low glycemic index chart. Sugar free may as well say, *fake everything else*. No sugar added may mean that there is enough in there naturally. Artificial sweeteners are killing small animals in cages, but maybe we are fine! Keep in mind that a high sugary diet leads to heart disease, and FM will make heart disease worse. Also keep in mind, anytime fat is removed, sugars are usually added. Another fun nutrition fact is that most veggies are fat soluble, and when you eat foods low in fat, your body is not processing the essential vitamins and minerals found in veggies as efficiently as it could be. You need *good* fats.

Splenda contains sucralose, and has small amounts of chlorinated pesticides and is currently my second favorite choice for sweeteners. Stevia brand sweetener is the only sweetener I can say I support as fibro friendly. Stevia rates at the top of the list for artificial sweeteners. Artificial sweeteners in general can cause joint and muscle pain, hormone imbalances, and cognition issues.

Most Sushi is bad, but it pretends to be good. Most sushi is super high on the glycemic index and filled with carbs, high in calories, and not as much protein as you would think. I will give it the benefit it does deserve, being loaded up with selenium, calcium, and Omega 3 fish oils, but remember what we think we know about food cancelling each other out? Crab meat usually is not even crab. It is a paste with crab cologne sprayed on it.

Peanuts can be good and bad. They come loaded with protein, magnesium, arginine, vitamin E, fiber, copper, and folate, all of which aid cardio health. But they are very high in fat and calories, and mega doses of Omega 6 (which needs to be balanced with Omega 3 to be considered healthy). Research has shown that peanuts are mostly contaminated by a carcinogenic mold known as aflatoxin, and they are in the top three most contaminated crops (usda.gov). Almonds are a healthy alternative to peanuts. That moves us on to peanut butter, while high in essential monounsaturated fats, most peanut butters are comprised of the same sugar as cake frosting. Eat nuts in small amounts.

Corn oil may seem harmless, but it has over fifty times the amount of Omega 6 than Omega 3, which increases inflammation and your risk for cancer, arthritis, and obesity. Walnuts, fish, and flaxseed have balanced Omega 6/Omega 3 ratios which is critical. Soy has been linked to increased estrogen in males, and increased breast cancer in women. Also, children have adverse developmental progress when consuming soy. *And*, here is the kicker for us FM health nuts—soy increases hypothyroidism, thyroid cancer, and infertility, among many others. Since there is a large number of us with FM that have hypothyroidism, it may make sense to avoid this one entirely. All those hippie vegans may want to switch back to another source of protein. Maybe try high protein foods like brown rice, goat's milk, coconut milk, almond milk, whole grains, nuts, seaweed, seeds, beans, and lentils. (Goat milk is suggested to be one of the healthiest foods there is).

Most yogurts are missing the mark. When manufacturers add fruit to yogurt, they also add corn syrup, which more than doubles the sugar value. Activia brand yogurt is a good alternative for its nutritional value as well as for its presence of live acidophilus, which promotes the proper yeast growth in your gut/digestive system. Since a large number of FM sufferers have IBS, leaky gut syndrome, and general digestive issues, balancing your yeast matters. Additionally, the presence of the probiotic saccharomyces is important as well for gut flora, not just acidophilus.

Diet soda is cancer concealed in a can, but it is better than sugared soda, right? Caffeine is okay for healthy people, but we tend to crash hard after a dose of caffeine—plus it accelerates your heart. The fructose portion of refined sugar is a building block for cholesterol. Some processed white flour, corn syrup offenders are pretzels, croutons, granola, English muffins, bagels, pasta salad, and white pastas—poor nutrition too—all low in protein, fiber, vitamins and minerals (high in carbs). Eat 100 percent whole grain or whole wheat pasta and English muffins to increase your protein and fiber. Egg salad is high in protein. Almonds are high in Omega 3 fatty acids.

No one wants to hear that they are eating poorly and further have to stop eating things they have always eaten and love. It is a little scary to think of eating like a cave man with so many in your face temptations that exist today. Let's face it though, we have an illness that makes us hypersensitive to a number of things, nutrition being at the top of the list. If you want to get well, you cannot ignore nutrition.

THE ELIMINATION DIET FOR FIBROMYALGIA

While elimination diets may have been originally designed to determine what food allergies you may be experiencing, they are also valuable in determining what foods irritate your chronic condition, like fibromyalgia, MCS, or IBS. The diet is pretty much like it sounds. You eliminate certain food groups, ingredients, or just about everything from your diet, and slowly and precisely, you reintroduce foods back into your diet every few days, and wait to see what irritates you, makes you sick, or causes flares.

An elimination diet can be very difficult. Like most other diets, they have an emotional and psychological effect on people, they are hard to follow, and they can result in a backfire for many people. After all, you will likely be eliminating your favorite foods, all the comfort foods, and be eating a stone-aged diet for several weeks which can be boring and frustrating. The eight most common offenders of food allergies are: eggs, fish, milk, peanuts, shellfish, soy, tree nuts, and wheat so consider starting with those if you think you may have sensitivities.

But the usual suspects for diseases like celiac disease, MCS, IBS, metabolic disorder, hyperglycemia, hypoglycemia, hypercholesterolemia, eating disorders, diarrhea, migraine, type II diabetes, mood disorders, depression, anxiety, anemia, nutrient deficiencies that lead to disease, hypertension, Crohn's disease, general digestive disorders, FM, CFS, and many more are: Simple carb sugars like: white sugar, white flour, white rice, white bread, cookies, cake, candy, breadsticks, pizza, soda, diet soda, mashed potatoes, baked potatoes, corn, cereal, pasta, spaghetti, bananas, carrots, mangoes, instant oatmeal, watermelon, dried fruit, orange juice, fruit juices, raisins, baked beans, pinto beans, navy beans, kidney beans, fava beans, black beans, potato chips, corn chips, ice cream, anything fried, pizza, tacos, tortillas, tobacco, alcohol, and high fructose corn syrup, and many more. If you eliminate the usual suspects listed above, you will be certain to see some wellness benefits and possibly some symptom relief. If nothing else, you will see weight loss. Carbs can promote inflammation, MCS, fatigue episodes and crashing, increased blood glucose levels, and yeast infections. Yeast due to MCS, allergies, and bowel disturbances can exacerbate joint pain and inflammation.

Gluten due to MCS, allergies, bowel and digestive disturbances can exacerbate gluten intolerance in some people. Nitrates, often found in lunchmeats, bacon, sausage, and hot dogs can exacerbate MCS, and bowel issues. Nightshade plants like: bell peppers, chili peppers, eggplant, potatoes, and tomatoes may exacerbate FM symptoms and promote inflammation and arthritis symptoms, but is unlikely for most people.

Caffeine can exacerbate fatigue flares, headaches, and disturbed sleep cycle. Avoid coffee, tea, soda, and chocolate. Avoid sweeteners like aspartame (an excitotoxin), and saccharine because they exacerbate pain and FM symptoms, headaches, and fatigue. Avoid carbonated drinks that cause metabolic reactions, which cause spikes in blood sugar. Rises and drops in blood sugar, as seen when eating sugary foods, exacerbate fatigue, and promotes carb cravings. If you have MCS or food intolerances, taking some medications like NSAIDS can break down your stomach lining, exacerbating these conditions. NSAIDS can also worsen your absorption of some vitamins and minerals.

TRIGGER FOODS

As with anyone in the world, the right diet will keep you healthier and living longer as a rule. A poor diet leads to disease. A poor diet can also add to mitochondrial dysfunction promoting fatigue. This is the area of the cell where energy is made. When you have FM, you are already living on the nutrition edge since your body will not process all foods as it should, depriving you of essential vitamins and minerals you may not even know you are missing. Eliminating these foods and then slowly reintroducing them back into your diet can be the key to discovering what foods you may be sensitive to. It is important to have a good multivitamin supplement with trace minerals, among other things like: Omega 3 fatty acid, flax seed, walnuts, fortified cereals, and eggs. Eggs can positively impact inflammation.

Items to avoid:

> Aspartame should be avoided as it is an excitotoxin that helps to stimulate the event known as NMDA (pain receptor).
>
> MSG/Food Additives should be avoided since they are suggested to intensify pain symptoms and also are

excitotoxins. Plus, the neurotransmitter glutamate is typically increased in fibro patient's already.

Sugar/fructose/simple carbs should be avoided since these sugars add to pain, exacerbate fatigue, increase energy crashes, add to weight gain, hypoglycemia, and diabetes.

Carbonated beverages should be avoided since they cause a metabolic reaction resulting in sugar pouring into the blood quickly. Causes a quick rise in blood sugar followed by subsequent fall that exacerbates fatigue.

Caffeine should be avoided because it causes a boost then collapse, exacerbating fatigue.

Yeast and gluten should be avoided. Yeast fosters the overgrowth of yeast fungus exacerbating muscle and joint pain. Gluten can exacerbate gluten intolerance resulting in a variety of stomach ailments and digestive issues. Remember, if you have FM, you are broken, and are likely to have more health issues in general. This may not be an issue for you though, as it only affects a percentage of FM sufferers.

Dairy like milk can drive the flu-type fibro symptoms upward in some people.

Night shade plants like tomatoes, chili and bell peppers, potatoes, and eggplant can trigger flares.

SUPPLEMENTS THAT TREAT FIBROMYALGIA

I have been around the block in the FM neighborhood. I have tried many trial and error protocols, most of which did not work for me, and many of which have no medical merit period. There are a lot of theory based protocols and I suggest trying whatever makes sense to you, starting with the easiest and cheapest if money is tight. The thing to remember with many chronic illness symptoms is that you will likely stumble onto relief in the form of *combinations* of drugs or therapies. If you have FM, you may want to try to establish a supplemental baseline that begins with something like the following: a multivitamin with trace minerals, vitamin D3, probiotics including acidophilus and saccharomyces, fish oil (1000 mg) or flaxseed oil (1200 mg) with 75 percent or more Omega 3, (Omega 3 has anti-inflammatory properties), magnesium (500mg) or to bowel tolerance, (slow magnesium is better yet), fiber (25mg), DHEA (25mg) for adrenal support, something to address sleep like melatonin (3mg), at least until you have established a sleep cycle.

The National Center for Complementary and Alternative Medicine (NCCAM) makes recommendations of herbs and supplements for average people with average health. At some point in your life, something went wrong that contributed to you being sick, and for many of us, our lifestyle in general may have taken us from sick to disabled. We just do not know the causes of FM, and to recover, we have to have an open mind and consider that many things made us sick, so many positive efforts may make us better. Below is a list of vitamins, minerals, and supplements that may have some wellness value for FM.

Calcium helps nerve and muscle function.

Capsaicin relieves muscle and joint pain by blocking pain sensitivity.

Cayenne aids in digestion and heart health.

Coenzyme-Q-10 has cardiovascular and antioxidant properties, controls oxygen flow to cells, helps in energy production, cognition, and mental function.

Colostrum helps immune system, and aids in infection.

D-Ribose enhances energy production, and aids in heart disease. D-Ribose is a pentose carb that helps to restore depleted energy stores in the tissue. It can restore energy and promote healthy cells in the heart and skeletal muscles. It can decrease pain, stiffness, and fatigue and can improve sleep and mental sharpness.

Echinacea increases your ability to resist infection and regulates energy production.

Ginger is a pain and inflammation reducer.

Kava is a sleep aid, muscle relaxant, and anxiety reducer.

Lavender relieves anxiety, insomnia, and depression.

L-Carnitine helps pain relief and improves mental health.

Magnesium aids in cellular activity, nerve, and muscle function, relaxation, anti stress, decreases fatigue, and increase pain tolerances.

Malic Acid helps muscle function, reduces pain, aids in metabolism, and raises energy levels.

Manganese helps with central nervous system function, coordination issues, nausea, and dizziness.

Melatonin is naturally found in our bodies. It improves sleep patterns, and regulates our sleep cycle and internal clock.

Milk Thistle is excellent for natural heart health.

Phosphorus helps with CNS, energy production, appetite, and insomnia.

Potassium helps with muscle function and nerve impulses.

Probiotics help with digestion and absorption.

5HTP is a building block for serotonin which helps depression and sleep.

Valerian is a pain reliever and tranquilizer.

Vitamin A maintains and repairs muscles.

Vitamin B1 helps with heart health, metabolism, formation of red blood cells, and maintains muscle.

Vitamin B6 helps in metabolism, hormone, neurotransmitter production, and immune system support.

Vitamin B12 helps in metabolism, iron absorption, formation of new cells, and decreases fatigue.

Vitamin C is an antioxidant and helps with stress.

Vitamin E helps with relaxation, is an antioxidant, aids in cognition, and stress control.

Zinc helps with cell growth and repair, immune system, and helps in vitamin absorption.

Any of the above has the potential to interact with other drugs.

DRUGS COMMONLY USED FOR FIBROMYALGIA

DOPAMINE AGONISTS

Dopamine agonists are like neurotransmitters that work on dopamine receptors by stimulating them in the brain, not adding dopamine to the body. It can trick the body's supply of dopamine into working where it may not currently be doing so. Dopamine affects brain processes that control things like pain, pleasure, emotions, and movement, etc.

Until recently, dopamine was used mostly for Parkinson's disease. Requip and Mirapex are two drugs that treat restless legs syndrome, which is commonly seen in FM. Dopamine is the neurotransmitter directly linked to the CNS and the adrenal glands so you can begin to see the relationship and dysfunction between the organs and glands. This same neurotransmitter that wreaks havoc in Parkinson's appears to be directly impacting areas of the brain in FM patients.

ANTI-ANXIETY

Anti-anxiety drugs like Paxil, Prozac, Valium, Xanax, Zoloft, Ativan, Cymbalta, Klonopin, Lexapro, etc. are commonly used to treat FM. Medication is likely not going to cure the issue long-term, but hopefully your anxiety is only acutely caused by your FM flares and is controllable.

Anxiety can be a slippery slope that can perpetuate your FM and is one of those symptoms that should not go on untreated. There are so many different types and brands of drugs available, you will likely have to work with your physician on a trial and error basis to find one that works well to suit your specific needs.

The side effects of these drugs can be risky as well and you may not realize when they occur as they can be related to your personality and may not be apparent to you. They can be addictive, but that should not stop you from seeking the treatment. Cognitive behavioral therapy would likely be a good alternative for anxiety and panic attacks, as you can learn behavioral modifications that will provide solutions or alternatives. My thinking is that if your anxiety is significant, you begin with medication to get it under control and transition into alternative therapies and out of the medication therapies. Below is a list of anti-anxiety drugs.

Prozac is a selective serotonin reuptake inhibitor (SSRI) used to treat fibromyalgia. Prozac is also used to treat depression, anxiety disorders, obsessive-compulsive disorder (OCD), bulimia, and premenstrual dysphoric disorder. Xanax is used to treat FM and the panic and anxiety symptoms associated with panic disorder. Xanax is a benzodiazepine which acts on the brain and CNS and produces a calming effect. It works by enhancing the effects of GABA, a natural chemical found in the body. Cymbalta is FDA approved to treat FM and is used to treat major depression and anxiety. In addition, Cymbalta is used to relieve nerve pain (peripheral neuropathy) in people with diabetes.

Lexapro is an SSRI used to treat FM, depression, and anxiety. It works by restoring the balance of neurotransmitters, such as serotonin in the brain. Lexapro may improve your feelings of well-being and energy level and decrease nervousness. Paxil is an SSRI used to treat FM, depression, panic attacks, obsessive-compulsive disorder, anxiety disorders, post-traumatic stress disorder, and premenstrual dysphoric disorder.

Klonopin is used to treat seizure disorders and panic attacks. Zoloft is an SSRI used to treat FM, depression, panic attacks, obsessive compulsive disorders, post-traumatic stress disorder, social anxiety disorder, and premenstrual dysphoric disorder. Valium is used to treat FM, anxiety, acute alcohol withdrawal, and seizures. It is also used to relieve muscle spasms and to provide sedation before medical procedures. Ativan is used to treat anxiety and is a benzodiazepine.

Retrieved from: http://www.healthcentral.com/anxiety/find-drug.html

SLEEP MEDS

Sleep is likely one of our biggest complaints just below pain and fatigue. Sleep may also be our primary perpetuating factor that affects other symptoms that plague us. Sleep medications may put one person to sleep and keep another one awake. These drugs should be used on a trial and error basis with your physician as well to try to find what works for you. Below is a list of some sleep aids that may work for you. There are numerous other sleep medications I have not listed here as I do not think they provide much value to FM. I do however think the use of melatonin is a good alternative to some of the prescription strength drugs, is inexpensive, and has no side effects.

Prozac, Zoloft, and Paxil are SSRI's and are used for pain management, depression, and sleep. Sometimes SSRI's are given in combination with tricyclic antidepressants, (TCA's) making them more effective against FM symptoms, although SSRI's have a preferable side effect profile versus TCA's. Sinequan and Nortriptyline are tricyclic antidepressants used to treat anxiety, depression, and sleep in FM. Flexeril and Soma are muscle relaxant's and are similar acting to tricyclic antidepressant's to improve sleep. They also work to reduce pain.

Klonopin is a benzodiazepine seizure medication that helps control restless legs syndrome, anxiety, and sleep in FM. It works to decrease electrical activity in the brain. Ambien is a sedative that treats insomnia and also works to slow brain activity. Ambien is said to restore deep sleep where many other drugs cannot. The bottom line here is that once you can get your sleep patterns under control, you should transition off of them and on to a regular sleep routine when possible.

MELATONIN

Melatonin is produced in the pineal gland in the brain and is secreted at night. It essentially helps to regulate the sleep cycle naturally, among other things. I recommend the synthetic delayed release products. When you have FM, you are likely not getting enough sleep, as well as having a disruptive sleep schedule (sleeping day and night). When this happens, you throw off your biological sleep clock and you can experience a number of FM type symptoms. Taking melatonin before bed can help to reset your clock. Since your immune system can be impacted with FM, taking melatonin can help to restore some immune function as well.

ANALGESICS

Analgesics/opioids are painkillers ranging from basic drugs like Tylenol to prescription medicines, such as Tramadol, and even stronger narcotics like Vicodin, Percocet, Oxycontin, Morphine, Dilaudid and Fentanyl. Typically for FM sufferers, even the strongest narcotics only take the edge off. There is no accepted research data established yet that shows that narcotics actually work to treat the chronic pain of FM; and the results are in-there is just not that much that works for us. My advice is finding other things that work and save this as a last resort and use them only on your worst days.

NONSTEROIDAL ANTI-INFLAMMATORY DRUGS (NSAIDS)

NSAID's like Aspirin, Ibuprofen, Advil, Naproxen, and Aleve, are used to treat inflammation. Inflammation is not typically an issue in FM, but NSAIDs also relieve pain too, and do help in some people with FM. Prostaglandins are the substances in the body that play a role in pain and inflammation, and can be inhibited by NSAID's. These help to alleviate some muscle aches, menstrual cramps and headaches often seen in FM sufferers.

ANTIDEPRESSANTS

Antidepressants are thought to be the most useful of meds in FM, typically in higher dosing than you may see otherwise. While depression is no more prevalent in FM than in any other chronic illness, these drugs are said to work either way because they elevate the levels of serotonin and norepinephrine in the brain that are separate from depression and function on pain and fatigue. Higher levels of these neurotransmitters are known to reduce pain in FM sufferers.

Tricyclic antidepressants have been suggested to provide some relief for FM symptoms in the form of restorative sleep, muscle relaxation, and decreased pain. You will likely receive a higher dose than those used to treat depression alone. Some examples are: Amitriptyline hydrochloride (Elavil, Endep). Cyclobenzaprine (Cycloflex, Flexeril, Flexiban), Doxer (Adapin, Sinequan), and Nortriptyline (Aventyl, Pamelor)ve Amitriptyline and Cyclobenzaprine have been proven ically in treating fibromyalgia. scribed

Selective serotonin reuptake inhibitors, (SSRr eated for the next step after tricyclics do not work. Thes; therefore in higher doses than versus individuals wh depression. These promote the releas reducing fatigue and other FM symptoms. SSRI's block the degradation (breakdown) of serotonin, allowing it to stay in the brain longer, increasing its effect. These drugs may include: Prozac, Paxil, Zoloft, Celexa, and Lexapro. Adding one of these drugs with a tricyclic antidepressant can work as a combination therapy. SNRI's or dual reuptake inhibitors are similar to TCA's and work on both serotonin and norepinephrine often producing less side effects and norepinephrine impacts the pain centers more than serotonin alone.

Mixed reuptake inhibitors are newer to the realm of FM therapy and have the capability of raising both the levels of serotonin and norepinephrine. These drugs may include Effexor, Cymbalta, and Savella. These combination drugs are a bit more effective on pain versus SSRI's, noted for their ability to raise norepinephrine, which likely contributes to a greater role in pain resistance than serotonin alone.

Benzodiazepines, like Clonazepam and Valium can be helpful for some neurological-like symptoms associated with FM. Restless leg syndrome and periodic leg movement disorder are neurological disorders that many FM suffers experience along the way. These drugs help to stabilize the nerve pathways from the brain that may become erratic, as well as tense, painful muscles, which add to the already poor sleep patterns. These drugs are thought to be highly addictive but addiction is not our greatest concern with life altering symptoms.

Another note on common misconceptions among medicines is bioidentical hormone replacement's. Bioidentical is a marketing term and is thought to have no scientific basis. Often hormones are plant based as are some synthetic hormones. synthetic hormone like Synthroid for thyroid dysfunction is is ured to resemble the human form of the hormone, and proved from non-plant based origins. Additionally, the labor pounding itself is not as safe or high quality as factured pharmaceuticals.

Complementary and alternative therapies have been documented to be helpful to most individuals who have truly given them an attempt. It can be what you make of it and if you half ass it, you will get only partial results. Controlled breathing has remarkable effects on chronic pain, anxiety, and various other symptoms. Gentle movement programs like yoga, Tai Chi, Reiki, Pilates, and the Feldenkrais method have positive, low invasive effects when done correctly. The National Center for Complementary and Alternative Medicine offers additional information.

The FDA does not regulate the sale or distribution of supplements, leaving information about actual affects, side effects, dosage, and active ingredients as unknowns. Many supplements are being studied for their effects on FM, it may however, be a long time before anything substantial surfaces. Most physicians do not know much about treating FM with conventional medicine, much less supplemental medicine.

WHAT DRUGS ARE RIGHT FOR ME?

You may have to do what myself and so many others have done with regard to drug therapy, which is to try everything you can until you find what works! While your doctor may not know what will work, or what order to attempt therapies in, you can always try what is easiest, cheapest, and least likely to kill you, as I was told at the Mayo Clinic.

The FDA has approved three drugs to treat FM: Cymbalta (Duloxetine), Lyrica (Pregabalin), and Savella (Milnacipran). Lyrica was approved in 2007 by the FDA and was developed to treat chronic pain caused by damage to the nervous system (neuropathic pain). Cymbalta was originally developed for depression, and Savella has been most recently approved for pain. Savella, like Cymbalta, acts as an anti-depressant increasing the neurotransmitters serotonin and norepinephrine in your brain (fda.org).

OPIOIDS—WHAT DO THEY REALLY DO AND WHY DON'T THEY WORK WELL FOR FIBROMYALGIA

Opioids, often called narcotics, come by many names. Quite simply for pain relief, they attach to opioid receptors (specific proteins) in the brain to block the perception of pain from the body, decrease the reaction to pain, and increase pain tolerance (opioid receptors are located in the brain, spinal cord, and GI tract). Nerves send and receive feelings of pain, and opioids stop this function. If the nerve message does not reach the brain, then you do not experience pain.

They also can provide antidepressant and calming effects for some people. The body produces its own endogenous, or natural opioids (similar to morphine), but your body will not produce enough natural opioid to combat the level of pain most often seen in chronic pain like fibromyalgia. An opioid acts as a neurotransmitter does, activating pain receptors. The brain does not differentiate between natural and synthetic opioids, thus the medicine will attach to nerves and activate them.

Opioids are chemically similar, but not identical to natural neurotransmitters, and eventually, the messages that are being sent to block pain become distorted or abnormal, leading to more pain. The message that gets sent is the neurotransmitter *dopamine*, which regulates cognitive functions, emotions, movement, motivation, and pleasure. So an opioid does not simply eliminate pain, it stops pain transmissions and alters the perception of pain.

The use of opioids to treat FM is debatable (as it is for many other chronic pain conditions). The primary reason opioids do not work well for fibro patients is that they are suggested to have a reduced binding ability of the pain receptors in the brain that most opioids target, meaning the drug will likely not work or work less than it should. Plus, it is believed that people with fibro have higher levels of endogenous opioids already, so taking meds like Vicodin can exacerbate pain. This area of the brain is known as the limbic system and is comprised of the thalamus, hippocampus, nucleus accumbens, formix, cingulate gyrus, and the amygdala. When painkillers cannot bind to the receptors, they cannot alleviate pain.

Positron emission tomography (PET) scans reveal that fibromyalgia patients have a reduced number of mu-opioid receptors. These pain receptors process pain messages. Reduced receptors translate into increased pain. So when you take opioids for pain relief, there are less receptors to bind to and reduce pain (other chronic pain conditions can have similarly reduced pain receptors). Additionally, the reduced number of opioid receptors means a reduced release of our natural (endogenous) opioids, like endorphins. PET scans also revealed that there are a reduced number of mu-opioid receptors in the amygdala region of the brain, resulting in an increase in depression and mood disorders- that may result in more pain.

Central Sensitization is the issue that FM sufferers have that puts us in a different category of pain than the rest of the world. Our bodies just do not work the same as people without FM, and thus standard pain killers do not work the same on us.

DEALING WITH SOCIAL SECURITY
OR DISABILITY

At some point you may need to deal with disability insurance or Social Security for income while you are incapable of working. It can be a difficult process while you have FM, especially if that is your only diagnosable illness. The state's Office of Disability Adjudication and Review (ODAR), may likely be looking for a more tangible diagnosis than FM, and it may take you every bit as long as two years or more to get a court hearing before you get to speak to an administrative judge regarding your health and disability.

Your best bet is to retain an attorney or service agency like *Allsup* to help expedite the Social Security process. Depending upon your state laws, an attorney or servicer may only be legally able to claim up to a specific amount of your settlement/claim that you are awarded, in many cases it can be as little as $4500, one time—typically not one-third of your settlement.

The bottom line here is that this process can be very taxing on your already overtaxed system. The process IS lengthy, complicated, and I would say that it is designed to force a percentage of people to quit the process due to difficulty of getting through the process itself. You may need help with the process, and you are allowed to have help every step of the way, even if it is a friend or family member who just has it together a bit better than you do. Keeping in mind how FM can wear you down cognitively, you may want help filling out this important documentation.

Make copies of each document you fill out before you send it to the state, because you may need to refer to what you wrote last time on the next document they send you; because they will send you redundant, overlapping documentation for review and to re-sign or to fill out again, and sometimes again.

Take each phone call from your Social Security representative and make calls when asked to in the documentation. Always keep your information in a well-organized file in a safe, consistent location that you can access each time you need to over the duration of the two years or so. Write notes each time of who you talked to, at what time and what date and what was said, and what they expect from you. Their job is very routine for them, but what they are going to ask of you will not be routine to you, so keep notes. Consider that you may be subject to investigation during this whole process, and that anything goes. This information applies to long-term disability insurance as well.

It is my belief that you will always have fibro and may always have some degree of symptoms. That being said, the day you decide to accept your illness, take control of your illness, create a wellness plan, and stop being the victim as I illustrate here, is the day you can set a goal date of exiting the Social Security system. I am not saying don't use Social Security, I did, and I planned on being on Social Security temporarily. I want you to evaluate your situation and decide if you should expect to be on disability temporarily, or forever, because the choice is yours and yours alone.

MANAGING CHRONIC PAIN
AND RETURN TO WORK

It is a major challenge to return chronic pain patients to work today and often is unsuccessful. After two years off on disability for fibro, lupus, or a related illness, you are only one percent likely to return to work, statistically. But chronic pain research and treatment is improving and this number can only go up. This presents a huge challenge for the patient. Often in typical cases a functional capacity evaluation (FCE) is performed by your employer to determine the extent of objectivity in symptoms. Typically then the patient participates in occupational therapy from home, which teaches the patient effective coping strategies.

The patient will attend psychological counseling the whole time the other strategies are in place. And finally, the patient is introduced back to work with a schedule they can handle, where applicable. This management program is suggested to take six months on average, and longer in some cases depending upon pain severity. Patients who experience chronic pain and do not return to work as expected have a major impact on not just the patient, but society as well. So there are challenges that will throw up brick walls with getting back to work, but these challenges can be mitigated and strategies for effectively returning to work are possible.

SYMPTOMS OF FIBROMYALGIA

Remember, your body is yours, kind of but that is not entirely true with FM, at least from a standpoint of the level of control you have over it going forward. The body acts and reacts completely different now that you have FM so everything matters going forward. There are going to be many things that you do not have control over, so it is pretty important to put as much effort into those factors you can control, even if its partial control.

By the time you get diagnosed with FM you may have more symptoms than the FM books say are catalogued symptoms for the illness. Keeping in mind that body systems work together and depending on what your body's response to your specific set of symptoms are can determine what *other* illnesses, disorders, and additional symptoms will begin to present.

Also keep in mind that there can be an unlimited number of factors in your life that are perpetuating your symptoms and this is extremely important in your recovery. Those factors can be stress and anxiety, diet, hygiene, fitness and cardiovascular health, and even environmental factors. Most people with FM have other illnesses or conditions too.

Some factors are never a good idea when you have FM due to the typical nature of the impacts on your symptoms. Things like alcohol, soda, high carb foods like cakes, cookies, and candy, can be perpetuating dietary factors that lead to flares. Don't forget exercising, hard work, and leading a normal life. Just existing can be challenge enough without eating foods or doing activities that force flare-ups.

Almost everyone with advanced FM shares the same core symptoms as their primary complaints. Pain almost always holds the first spot with fatigue a close second. The lack of restorative sleep seems to be a common denominator with varying degrees of severity. These three symptoms alone can be disabling so find a way to manage or eliminate these, even a little bit at a time, through your wellness program and preventative methods; keeping your *illness baseline* higher, and your additional symptoms stable.

The idea that you will get less quality sleep perpetuates numerous other factors in your body leading to many other symptoms. It seems that with FM, no matter how much sleep you get, you will likely awaken just as tired as when you fell asleep, and often have no sense of achieving a *refreshed* sleep; one that heals the body, rejuvenates the mind and soul, and charges the batteries. Many FM sufferers will sleep 10 hours and feel like they slept 15 minutes, awaken tired and un-refreshed, and biologically have achieved 30 minutes of *deep sleep*.

These symptoms are not all inclusive of FM and may overlap many illnesses.

SYMPTOMS

Generalized pain/stiffness in muscles and joints, every muscle can ache, throb or pulse simultaneously, or intermittently. Pain is everywhere else. The pain and fatigue typically can present like a roller coaster.

Joints are popping mostly after rest.

Generalized fatigue or severe episodes of fatigue. Delayed fatigue. CFS.

Frequent infections.

Addison's disease, secondary adrenal insufficiency.

Generalized flu-like feeling, radiating body pain, super fatigue, extreme tiredness, nausea, headache, body shakes, body aches. Morning sickness, hangover feeling.

Frequent headaches.

Myofascial pain.

Cognitive impairment, concentration issues, word confusion and recall issues, sensory stimulus issues, multi-tasking issues. Fibrofog, memory issues in general, dyslexia type issues.

Sleeping disorders, extreme sleepiness, apnea, insomnia.

Vertigo, dizziness, coordination, balance, swaying issues.

Electricity sensations, you experience electric type stimulations, and feel it in your muscles, numbness, tingling.

Inability to lose weight, increased appetite, extreme junk food cravings, carbohydrate cravings.

Exercise intolerance. No matter how much or how often you exercise your body seems resistant to the motions and the work. Typically you take days or weeks to recover after working out. You cannot make gains in strength, muscle tone, definition, or stamina/repetition.

Unrelenting dry eyes and mouth and skin. Polydipsia-excessive thirst.

Visual disturbances, blurred, tunnel vision, spotty vision, perception issues.

GERD, acid reflux, severe bloating after eating, abdominal pain, vomiting, nausea, metabolic issues.

Bladder dysfunction, frequent urination, overactive bladder. Alternating diarrhea and constipation. IBD.

Sporadic blood pressure, arrhythmias, irregular heartbeats, palpitations, shortness of breath, chest pain, other cardiac issues, drops in BP upon standing, MVP-mitral valve prolapse.

Sore throats, choking issues, difficulty swallowing.

Loss of libido, sexual dysfunction, painful sexual organs.

Menstrual issues in general.

Restless leg syndrome or periodic leg movement disorder.

Transient paralysis-difficulty initiating movement. Tremors.

Hair follicle hypersensitivity. Your hair is sensitive to the touch, hurts when rubbed or itched, and is irritated by clothes rubbing hair, itchy skin. Sensitive skin, skin rashes, tumors or lumps.

MCS-multiple chemical sensitivity, severe allergies, neuropathic issues, hypersensitivity to environmental odors, or the smell of diesel burn-off in front of you at an intersection, cleaning products, animal odors.

Inability to maintain regulated internal or external climates, low grade fever, intolerances to heat and cold, profuse sweating. Hormone issues in general. Thyroid disease.

TMJ-Temporomandibular joint, general jaw pain. Carpal tunnel syndrome

EBV-Epstein Barr Virus. HHV6-Human Herpes Virus 6.

Candida Albicans. Celiac disease.

Depression, anxiety, panic attacks, dramatic mood swings, intolerances to stress, emotional intolerances.

High cholesterol, high triglycerides.

COMORBIDITY: Viscous cycle disorders-the relationship between FM and other illnesses

This list is not conclusive of course, and continues to grow. Some of these symptoms are not directly related to FM.

RELATED ILLNESSES
AND COMORBIDITY

So you are wondering if your FM has caused your other symptoms/illnesses, or if your other symptoms/illnesses caused you FM? Since current medicine cannot really answer that question, let us assume for the moment that your primary illness is FM. It seems that nobody has FM only. Most people have myriad additional symptoms and/or diagnoses or abnormal test results that amount to nothing medically substantial. The reality is that fibro is the likely culprit for many of your unexplained symptoms.

Comorbidity is the culmination of all of your other symptoms or illnesses other than your primary illness. These comorbid factors can present on a spectrum and be independent of FM or in combination, but will all likely be perpetuating factors that must be dealt with. Whether these comorbid conditions are secondary or tertiary symptoms/illnesses, you will stand a much better chance for success if you can eliminate them one by one.

I have spent considerable time attempting to category and inventory my symptoms individually, looking for their source or root cause, and working to eliminate them any way I can. The fact remains that many of these symptoms form part of a cycle that is dependent upon other factors, and must be treated as a whole, or at least cannot be eliminated like items on a checklist.

Since there are very few standardized tests that help to identify root factors in the majority of the FM symptoms, often they are overlooked or misinterpreted as something else or nothing. And since you may have encountered at least one physician who is not equipped to appropriately treat or even identify FM and its many symptoms, it only adds to the viciousness of the cycles. Let us assume for the moment that you may not be able to isolate all of your symptoms independent of one another and figure them all out. This is a likely scenario. The next best thing is to keep looking for answers and keep accepting the treatments that are available to eliminate what you can eliminate. But, one thing is certain-you can reverse your illness to a much more manageable level if you follow what I have explained. In the end, when you have learned to manage your illness you will be left with pain, fatigue, and one or two more symptoms and these will be significantly reduced and manageable.

CFS: While the majority of FM sufferers will also meet the diagnostic criteria for CFS, there are subtle differences, even though some experts may argue they are synonymous. The two disorders share most of the same symptoms and respond similarly to similar treatments—which is not much at all. Fatigue seems to be the primary symptom of CFS, while pain is the primary symptom in FM.

Epstein Barr Virus: EBV is likely one possible underlying trigger of FM and CFS. It is an infection that never leaves the body and is said to be capable of reactivation, triggering FM. This virus is difficult to treat and even more difficult to eliminate from the body, making it a likely lifelong causal effect to FM.

Mononucleosis: Mono is a fairly common virus that first appears like FM. It is said to be caused by EBV and once you get it you will carry the virus for life and it may activate periodically, possibly not making you sick. The symptoms seem more on the line of the infection symptoms like a sore throat, fever, weakness, and fatigue. There is nothing really you can do, and it will go away on its own—typically.

Arthritis: Arthritis is a disease of the joint involving inflammation—one of the primary symptoms not typically found in FM. Physicians always look to rule out arthritis on their way to diagnosing you. Many people with FM also have some degree of arthritis, and many of those are treatable. There are over 100 types of arthritis identified so far.

Lupus: Lupus is an autoimmune disease where the immune system attacks the body. The symptoms can be overwhelming and the damage can be devastating. There is a known link to EBV and women are 9 times more likely than men to develop the illness. Like FM, it is said to be difficult to diagnose.

Lyme's Disease: Lyme's disease is likely the first thing your doctor will test you for when you come to him complaining of FM symptoms; at least to rule it out. It is a bacterium that comes from a tick bite and is fairly common in the United States. The first sign can be flu symptoms, much like FM, but you can also get fatigue, headaches, and pain. This can be treated with antibiotics in early stages and becomes chronic if not caught and treated early.

Sleep Disorders: Sleep disorders like snoring, insomnia, apnea, RLS, PLMD, etc., can mimic FM in early stages. Since sleep issues are a fundamental issue with FM, it is important to try to understand what is causing your sleep issue and attempt to address it where possible.

Severe Obesity: According to the CDC, if you weigh 20 percent more than your BMI you are obese. If you are over 50 percent overweight you are morbidly obese and this will likely interfere with the normal function of your body. This can be a problem with FM since we are moving less than we used to now that we have this illness.

Depression: FM does not cause depression. It is believed that you are no more likely to suffer from depression with FM than with any other chronic illness. That being said, psychological disorders like depression and anxiety often accompany chronic pain disorders. There is no causal link between the two, but there are a percentage of individuals in the medical field who do not differentiate between the two. Sadly, this leads to a delay in diagnosis and undermines public confidence.

Myalgic Encephalomyelitis (ME). The British name for FM is ME. Some people use the two interchangeably, but the name is not used that much in the US. Some degree of controversy surrounds this condition and very little funding in the United States is going to its research today. More is being done outside the United States and ME is considered a neuroimmune disease by some.

HHV-6: HHV-6 is an infection that can persist in the brain and contribute to fibrofog. It can play a role in CFS in conjunction with EBV. Elevated antibody titers do correlate with active infection. Studies have been published using tests that do not differ between active and latent infection. This is important so your doctor knows how or what to treat. Often, latent infections will present and can be triggers and it is unknown to what extent this happens or the likelihood.

Addison's disease: Addison's disease may be a contributing factor to FM as it may be linked to hypothalamus dysfunction and low cortisol. Addison's disease, at least the form seen in FM, is secondary adrenal insufficiency, as a result of pituitary gland dysfunction. Cortisol may be needed to address adrenal gland deficiencies as a result of pituitary gland dysfunction. This hormone helps physiologic stressors, maintains blood pressure, and reduces inflammation. It can have an effect on hypoglycemia as well. It aids in the energy producing process that supports brain function. Get checked for this.

Thyroid disease: Low thyroid in general has many of the same symptoms as FM. Hashimoto's Thyroiditis is an autoimmune disorder that is very prevalent in FM patients. It is the most common cause of hypothyroidism and is when the body attacks the thyroid gland as if it were foreign tissue. This plays a role in the adrenal function as well and is thought to be a main contributing factor to some of the viciousness of the FM cycles of illness. Get checked for this.

MPS: Chronic myofascial pain syndrome is a painful neuromuscular disease affecting sheaths of the muscles. MPS causes trigger points of pain, not unlike FM in some patients. Many patients have both MPS and FM at the same time, although both are suggested to be unrelated.

Candidiasis: A common yeast infection from a yeast overgrowth. Candida is commonly found in our body, and may not ever present a problem. In FM, there can be a build-up of yeast causing infection, leading to other factors.

Orthostatic intolerances: A disorder of the autonomic nervous system when blood pressure drops occur upon standing. This can be fairly typical in FM. Sometimes visual disturbances or blackouts can occur.

Dysautonomia: Dysautonomia is an autonomic nervous system dysfunction. A breakdown of many of your involuntary functions can occur with this disorder. There are a number of different types and severities of this condition that may affect FM.

Research has already proven that HHV-6, mycoplasma pneumoniae, chlamydia pneumonia, and Epstein Barr Virus among others may be involved in FM and CFS. Many of us have more than one of these issues and it seems easy to connect the dots and draw conclusions. I would imagine that soon, these may be on the list of underlying triggers in FM. Today, however, your physician cannot connect the dots between most abnormal labs like these and fibromyalgia. The reality is-something is triggering fibro to *begin*. We don't know what it is yet. You need to know what is separate from and related to your fibro to know if you should be managing your fibro *only* or addressing unrelated illnesses that are impacting or exacerbating your fibro.

LAB TESTING

The main reason FM is so misunderstood and misdiagnosed is largely due to the average physician's lack of knowledge on the subject. You can go years with the lack of a diagnosis simply because your doctor does not really know how to make a proper diagnosis. And you can go even longer after a diagnosis trying to figure out how to treat it, primarily because your doctor does not have a clue how to put the pieces of the puzzle together and draw effective conclusions from his findings. Today there is only so much information available between what we can do on our own and what the medical world can help us with. Plus, chronic illness symptoms are not accurately represented regardless of lab or imaging results.

In my case I went roughly sixteen years with a handful of test results that fell into the *slightly off* category, with absolutely no clue as to what to do about them. Every physician I saw was clueless at that point. I began to educate myself about the illness and continued to be rejected or scrutinized by numerous physicians. I was desperately looking for a physician who had done at least one puzzle before I arrived.

Much like many of you, I put more than my trust in my doctors; I put the fight of my life in their hands, and came up empty handed often. In our society, *physician* means so much more than successfully educated individuals, entrusted to heal mankind. These individuals are placed on pedestals and deemed experts, and whatever they say is considered fact. When you are chronically ill with symptoms that are a medical mystery, you hang on every word from your medical staff, every test result, every piece of advice, and you become familiar with rejection.

You use everything in your toolbox to gain something, anything that can help you in any way, to get back to some semblance of life pre-FM. Along the way, a little bit of you dies, and you realize you have not hit bottom yet. Hope is stripped away from us one doctor visit, one negative test result, or one non-empathetic person at a time, and it is up to us to find new hope. Finding that right doctor can mean the difference between sickness and wellness for you.

With FM you will often see variations in certain lab results that may not be a definitive answer to one thing or another. Having low iron, for example, can truly mean many different things, and it is difficult to know what the cause of unique lab results can be. To start with, your physician should at least run a complete blood count and the basic serum tests as well as a thyroid test and basic inflammation marker tests. With FM, you may experience low vitamin B6, B12, basal metabolic rate, DHEA, gamma globulin, magnesium, melatonin, pregnenolone, progesterone, testosterone, thyroid; as well as having varying lab results in: Cardio CRP, absolute eosinophils, absolute basophils, AST, ALT, growth hormone, EBV, immunoglobulin, lipoprotein, liver enzymes, natural killer cell, thrombin antithrombin, and angiotensin. Your cholesterol may be high as well—a number of factors can alter these numbers.

Your thyroid peroxidase levels may be too high. Overall thyroid function is low, caused by thyroid disease or Hashimoto's thyroiditis, which is also contributing to the difficulty in losing weight and gaining muscle. Your thyroid increases metabolism and controls weight, boosts blood circulation, keeps skin supple, soft, flexible, and warm, prevents hair loss, prevents loss of memory and concentration, and lowers cholesterol. Your doctor may recommend synthetic hormone replacement, but it is critical to have a complete thyroid picture to know exactly what hormone you need and in what dose. You may need a thyroid or T3/T4 hormone replacement for life.

Your cortisol may be low which affects your immune system, stress, appetite, energy, digestion, joint movement, inflammation, temperature, and mood, increases pain and fatigue, and aids in stabilization of blood sugar. You may be diagnosed with Hypothalamic-Pituitary-Adrenal Axis Dysfunction (HPA) possibly as a result of long-term pain. The HPA dysfunction that is present in most FM sufferer's results in HPA axis dysfunction that is often not detected by standard testing done in a clinical setting, as these tests are designed to detect primary adrenal insufficiency and have poor sensitivity for secondary or tertiary adrenal insufficiency. Additionally, HPA dysfunction results in secondary or tertiary hypothyroidism that is not detected with the standard thyroid test, (most doctors administer) and low growth hormone production that is also not detected by standard testing. Research has shown that boosting the thyroid in many of those with FM is beneficial, even when labs would suggest otherwise.

Research has also shown that HPA dysfunction is associated with mitochondrial dysfunction, sleep disorders, immune dysfunction, chronic infections, autonomic dysfunction, gastrointestinal dysfunction, and coagulation dysfunction in the same patients. The hypothalamus has significant pain modulating properties and hypothalamic dysfunction has been shown to increase pain sensation. Since the hypothalamus is the most complex part of the CNS, it lends credibility that much more research needs to be done specifically within this area. Bottom line, you are likely suffering from clinically significant adrenocortical dysfunction, and diagnosis is difficult.

First of all, your general practitioner is not going to order even half of the above tests for you. Most physicians cannot determine a proper translation of the data when these tests are conducted for FM, so they are not going to order the tests. This is part of the problem with FM diagnosis taking so long. Depending on who does order these tests, and how they are translated, will be the dividing line between illness and wellness. Not that everyone needs all of these tests ordered, but if you have had some of these labs done, an experienced physician can begin to put the puzzle together and know which direction to take your specific treatment.

Ranges that are developed in labs are inconclusive for most of what we suffer from having FM/CFS. Plus, ranges change from lab to lab, which proves that what you may think is a baseline may not be, and there are too many variables to provide skewness of the tests, which cause doubt in the minds of the physicians. Most of us will test slightly out of range, and your physician will likely do nothing about the results, thinking you are close to the range limits.

The average range is a snapshot of roughly two percent of the population, including the standard deviation. This just does not take into account those of us who test in the outer limits where FM patients usually test. So when your doctor orders a blood test to check your thyroid activity, they will typically check the TSH and T4, and disregard T3. So for example, FM falls into a category of diagnostic uniqueness when it comes to the thyroid, and must be observed more thoroughly than doctors typically test for.

If we take a look at neurochemical imbalances and FM, we can see what researchers are working on right now. One theory is that FM may be caused by the wrong amounts of certain neurochemicals in the brain and CNS. The nerves in your body connect to the brain, and when you have pain, that message is sent to the brain to let you know something hurts. The messages are the neurochemicals, and they need to maintain a delicate balance or the way you feel pain will be changed or misinterpreted. There are four neurochemicals in particular that are commonly imbalanced in the body of an FM sufferer: substance P, serotonin, glutamate, and dopamine.

Substance P's primary responsibility is to amplify pain signals in the body. Research has shown that many people with FM have two to three times the normal amount of this neurochemical versus a healthy person. This is where researchers believe that you may experience more pain than you should. You may be sensitive to the touch, your hair can hurt, and likely your whole body; and no one will know why, and objective evidence may not show why.

Serotonin is related to sleep, pain, and mood. These levels are typically low in FM, or the levels may be normal, but the chemical is not being used properly by the body. This is where antidepressants can help people with FM. In higher than normal doses, drugs like Prozac, Paxil, Zoloft, and Celexa can help the serotonin be used efficiently in the body.

Glutamate plays a role in excitatory signal transduction in the nervous system and is involved in cognition, memory, and learning-all fibrofog issues. Glutamate is involved in awareness, pain, brain development, and is found in higher than normal levels in those with fibro. High levels of glutamate over-stimulate brain cells causing malfunctioning neurons.

Dopamine is believed to be responsible for pain processing in the brain. When our bodies are stressed, which is all the time with FM, dopamine production is reduced in the brain, and this is where pain can be experienced at much higher levels than it should be. And in the long run, you produce less dopamine.

Another big mystery that surrounds FM is the HPA Axis dysfunction. As I noted earlier, there is something in us with FM that does not shut off the *fight-or-flight* response, overtaxing our system in many ways. The autonomic nervous system controls automatic mechanisms like digestion, breathing, blood pressure, and heart rate. During moments of stress, adrenaline and cortisol are released as mechanisms to help us mitigate a response to the stress, like running away from a black bear in the wild. Those of us with FM maintain slightly higher than normal levels of these stress hormones, as well as our systems taking longer to recover from an event, which is exhausting. Some of the symptoms we have often are acute symptoms that occur during a highly stressful event, like palpitations, labored breathing, sweating, and flulike feelings; but we can have these all the time and these symptoms throw physicians off the disease trail.

Chronic pain eventually can become that constant stressor that overtaxes our bodies day in and day out, since we cannot shut it off. In theory, long-term effects of this occurring cause's physical change in the brain, as it relates to the way pain signals are processed. Eventually this leads to us being overly sensitive or having multiple chemical sensitivities among other things; and these prolonged, untreated chronic illnesses overtime, can lead to additional illnesses and diseases, and psychological disorders.

WHAT IS THE RIGHT TREATMENT APPROACH FOR FIBROMYALGIA?

Often what you will find with fibro is that many people do not respond to *standard of care treatments*. These include what the majority of physicians and governmental bodies like the CDC, the NIH, and most importantly, the FDA agree with.

There are not as many disbelieving doctors out there as there used to be, but it is commonplace for many physicians to prescribe whatever Big Pharma is currently pushing for FM. This means that alternative treatments, supplements, and off-label use of medications may not be popular because they are not financially beneficial to those in the medical field, as well as considered safe for use. Some of the most prestigious medical journals in America will acknowledge that financial ties between Big Pharma and medical researchers have been a problem since the 1980s.

This suggests that many in the medical field prescribe what they are told to by Big Pharma, which would be contrary to medications that do not profit that industry like supplements, alternative treatments, off-label drugs used, and drugs that are out of patent protection. Also, physicians are required to gain continuing education units (CEU's) each year, of which, roughly 70 percent of physician's continuing education is paid for by Big Pharma, through free trips and junkets, and concealed payments.

So when you have tried several medications for fibro like Lyrica, Cymbalta, Savella, and a number of antidepressants and opioids, all with no positive benefit, and then you ask your physician for a script for low dose naltrexone because you have read a number of articles about its efficacy in treating fibro, and your physician says no—it may be due to the fact that this drug would be used off-label which may make your physician uncomfortable to prescribe, or it may be because the drug patent expired a long time ago and prescribing it is not profitable for anyone anymore! This is something to consider and reinforces what I suggest about finding the right doctor, and educating yourself so you know how to advocate for yourself when the time comes to.

I think the best choice of medicine for fibro is a combination of conventional and alternative medicine (complimentary medicine). This seems to be the logical choice for the individual, versus the majority, which seems necessary with many cases of fibro. Standard of care treatments certainly have their place in medicine, but when it comes to complex illness syndromes, like fibro, it just does not always work.

MY TREATMENT PROGRAM

I once had one physician draw 32 vials of blood, looking for just about everything. Many of the tests ordered were a first for me, reinforcing the idea that the doctors I had seen prior, did not believe me about my symptoms, or did not want to test me for some other unknown reason, delaying my diagnosis and treatment. The lab results showed that I was positive for more than 10 of the tests, and had another 10 severe vitamin or mineral deficiencies. FM was attributed to being the primary illness, and many additional factors played a role as well. The vicious cycle you keep hearing about comes to light when you factor in 20 plus symptoms with almost no medically significant test results to qualify them. It was not enough objective evidence.

Every doctor I had seen prior to that had no clue as to the extent of havoc FM can wreak, and furthermore those doctors' lack of knowledge about this illness in general may have very well lead to the degree of exacerbation of my symptoms and further the severity of my illness; not to mention the numerous other chronic illnesses that have since riddled my body. After all, I started out with pain and fatigue and felt slightly fluish some days, and soon had over 20 symptoms and eventually became disabled. My symptoms slowly began to add on as my body began malfunctioning from ineffective or absent treatment and misdiagnosis.

By that point, I was diagnosed with, of course, FM, but also with CFIDS, Hashimoto's Thyroiditis, Epstein Barr, HHV-6, HPA axis dysfunction, periodic leg movement disorder, sleep apnea, postural orthostatic tachycardia syndrome, dysautonomia, cardiomyopathy, neurogenic bladder, diverticular disease, GERD, connective tissue disease, high cholesterol, high blood pressure, candida, Addison's disease, chronic myofascial pain syndrome, inflammatory bowel disease, multiple chemical sensitivities, and significant deficiencies or malfunctions in: iron, magnesium, aldosterone, testosterone, cortisol, immunoglobulin G and M, pregnenolone, thyroid peroxidase, DHEA sulfate, ferritin, folate, cholesterol, HDL (good), LDL (bad), triglycerides, metabolic rate, lipoprotein, ALT, vitamin B6, thrombin-antithrombin TAT, IGF-1, angiotensin, TNF alpha, natural killer cell, and my homocysteine cardio CRP (risk) was high. I was a mess. I finally got a bit more medical attention after a stroke occurred from heart damage that was related to my untreated conditions. Two years prior to all of these symptoms/illnesses I was undiagnosed for everything except mild hypothyroidism.

Ninety-nine percent of these labs were never requested by any other doctors in seventeen years of complaining and perpetual illness. I had never received a diagnosis. I had never received proper treatment for any of these things, and I had never been taken seriously. I was treated for low thyroid, but with the wrong drug and dosage, and my hormone levels were never regulated. It is unbelievable that today, people still go through trial and error with doctors trying to just get better. But it was clear at that point that I had multiple possible underlying causes of my symptoms and that my body was not working correctly. The truth is it was refreshing to have a discovery like this—the worst part of this illness is not knowing. Finding out what the big picture is helps you to get your arms wrapped around the problem and focus on looking for solutions, and quit focusing on the problem. The more you know, the more you arm yourself with the tools to improve your situation.

I believe that underlying infections or imbalances that we all have may manifest during these periods in FM sufferers. The idea is to find a comprehensive approach to treating this illness as well as to treat the underlying causes of pain, fatigue, and immune deficiency.

With regard to underlying causes of FM, not much is really known at this point. There are, however, some interesting points for observation. For example, Epstein Barr Virus is said to have a causal relationship to FM. HHV-6 can disrupt the immune system by infecting white blood cells. It infects and destroys cells that make up *myelin*, which protects nerve cells. Mycoplasma pneumoniae can hide from the immune system and can cause infection in the brain and spinal cord. Chlamydophila pneumoniae may cause or exacerbate your symptoms. All of these issues can have a cause and effect relationship with FM. And all of these issues are prevalent in FM patients.

UNDERSTANDING CHRONIC PAIN

FM can cause significant disability, and the longer you have had it, especially untreated with proper medical care, the worse it can be. FM can make everything you do more difficult or in some cases impossible. Roughly 30 percent of FM sufferers will no longer be capable of working due to the chronic symptoms associated with the illness (rheumatology.org).

You have to understand the nature of pain, and how acute pain differs from chronic pain. As I began to thoroughly understand pain, I began to understand fibro better and I was more equipped to accept and cope with my situation. Acute pain is different from chronic pain in almost every way. From its etiology to its pathophysiology and to the way it is diagnosed and treated, the way you experience pain, how it shows up on x-rays, neuroimaging, tests, and in your labs. Pain will tell you if you are seriously injured or not. How the body processes pain is fairly complicated, that is one reason why there are so many different types of pain drugs on the market. Pain may be the chief symptom or perpetuating factor in FM, never allowing your body to heal itself. If you do not control the pain to some degree, it will control you.

Another difficult thing about treating or curing FM is that it is a biochemical disorder that affects your whole body. No one has FM in just one area. This tricky fact is part of the accuracy of the diagnosis itself. If you do not have whole body pain, you have something else entirely. This is why a clinical history is so important in making the diagnosis. And while your chief complaint may be something else, you could still have FM, and FM could become a perpetuating factor to your primary illness.

Chronic pain can be classified as nociceptive or neuropathic. Acute pain is more nociceptive providing a protective biological function which warns us when something is wrong, whereas chronic pain provides no biological function and is suggested to be a disease of its own. Nociceptive pain is caused by the activation of nociceptors. Neuropathic pain is caused by damage or a malfunction to the nervous system. Neuropathic pain originates in the peripheral nervous system, brain or spinal cord (helpforpain.com). Different types of painkillers target these different types of pain. Pain can be further divided and described in greater detail, but for the purpose of FM I will keep it as basic as possible.

Pain activates nociceptors that carry the information to receptors that essentially create a signal for pain. The majority of the information is first transported to the thalamus, whose role is to relay the messages between the brain and the parts of the body. After that the pain signal moves to the limbic system where our emotions are processed, and then to the cortex where complicated thoughts are formulated. In FM, this cycle never shuts down and runs constantly. It is suggested that over time, pain alters the brain and nervous system, and physically changes them, even causing premature aging and degeneration. Chronic pain, then, is progressive and degenerative. The physical alterations that occur in the brain may lead to fibrofog among many other things and actual brain damage occurs from chronic pain. This will hopefully be one of those *real* fact based bits of research that puts FM in a more credible classification soon.

Disorder Sensory Processing is what FM does to the body. The problem with chronic pain is the linear relationship between nociception and pain is inappropriate or absent and the expected recovery does not occur. Most of us FM sufferers have unique pain which is not helped much if at all by most painkillers. The source of the pain is typically the target most physicians are aiming for, but with FM our pain is mostly central, not out in the periphery, and difficult to pinpoint, therefore difficult to extinguish. The way strong pain killers like narcotics target pain is somewhat insignificant in FM and many people feel no pain relief at all. The body produces its own pain relieving chemical *endorphins* in a person without FM—but we have a malfunction in this process. For example, narcotics attach to the endorphin receptors and typically provide no relief for us. Exercise among other things causes the body to produce these endorphins naturally without the use or overuse of medications that are likely to cause other issues or serious side effects.

PAIN RECEPTORS

Pain starts with nerves. Pain receptors are found on nerve endings throughout the body in your skin, muscles, joints, connective tissues, and internal organs. Pain receptors become activated as a response to painful stimuli. These stimuli may involve trauma or injury, but in the case of fibromyalgia, where pain states like *hyperalgesia* and *allodynia* are present, the stimulus may be very mild or nothing at all.

Pain receptors release neurotransmitters when they become stimulated, which send pain messages to the brain and spinal cord, via the nerves. What was just described is called *nociception*, since the pain receptors in question are called nociceptors. The damaged or affected tissue in question releases second messengers including bradykinin, prostaglandins, histamine, serotonin, leukotrienes, and potassium.

Pain medications have the ability to inhibit, or reduce some of these pain transmissions. When this happens, the pain receptors can potentially not be activated—making the pain impulse incapable of reaching the brain and the perception of pain is reduced or more likely eliminated. The afferent nerve fibers (two types: A-delta and C-sensory fibers) are the peripheral nerve fibers that contain pain receptors. These send nerve impulses (pain messages) back to the brain and spinal cord. Multiple sclerosis affects the A-delta fibers, known as myelinated nerves, which produce somatic pain, typically arising out of damage to the skin or muscle. However, the C-sensory pain fibers respond to dull, achy, non-localized pain stimuli (unmyelinated). These typically respond to visceral pain, or internal pains to organs, etc.

When second messengers activate pain receptors, they send the pain stimulus along the afferent nerves to the dorsal horn in the spinal cord. These pain signals are then sent to various parts of the brain for a response. The last step in a pain transmission is the brain responding and telling the body how to react. These impulses move along the efferent nerves from the brain. At this point, many different substances may be released from the brain and spinal cord that impact the perception of pain (neurochemical mediators) of which includes endorphins-natural opioids, serotonin, and norepinephrine.

Pain medications and antidepressants acting as pain killers target these processes to address pain. The neurotransmitter glutamate is the dominant neurotransmitter when the threshold to pain is first experienced, and is associated with acute pain—pain that warns us that something is wrong. Substance P is a peptide that is released by C fibers and is usually associated with chronic pain. Glycine suppresses the pain transmission in the dorsal root ganglion, blocking the potential for pain or inflammation.

Neuropathic pain is pain caused by trauma or injury to the nerves from damage, inflammation, and tumors. *Visceral* pain is pain originating in the ANS's sensory neurons. This visceral pain is not felt in a discrete location as pain signals transmitted by the sensory-somatic system are.

So pain strikes, activating nociceptors near the injury site (or FM pain site), the nociceptors send a response (nerve impulse) through the spinal cord toward the brain. This happens in a fraction of a second. The spinal cord acts as a middle man in the pain transmission process most of the time, but can mitigate a response to some pain with reflexes.

The dorsal horn in the spine acts as a central hub for information. So some responses come from the brain, and some from the dorsal horn; the brain does most of the work though. The brain makes sense out of the injury, cataloging the pain (checking for memory of that pain), and gearing up to make a response. Pain signals first arrive at the thalamus in the brain where it gets directed for interpretation. The thalamus sends signals to the cortex and limbic system. Then the cortex compares the pain to previous pain and determines its origin. The limbic system releases an emotional response (like crying, or sweating, etc.). This is a critical mechanism in chronic pain conditions. Perineuronal nets are created with a survival function to reduce our future impact to chronic acute pain. Here we have an opportunity to understand pain and to train our brain to recognize certain pain and react normally to it versus to overreact to it—crippling us from that pain. Perineuronal nets preserve our important protective pain memories but still allow neuroplasticity to occur-making new memories and physically changing our brain. With fibro, we may be experiencing permanant changes from incorrect connections.

Pain is not a simple cause and effect system. It is impacted by everything occurring in your nervous system including mood, past experiences, expectations, and many things that can influence the way you experience or perceive pain. You may have a higher pain tolerance than someone else as a result of previous pain experiences.

Acute pain is eliminated when the injury has healed, as a rule, and the nociceptors no longer detect damage or injury. BUT, when pain receptors continue to fire as a result of disease or illness causing damage, (even in the absence of damage as seen in fibro) pain signals are traveling to the brain constantly. The cause of the pain has been eliminated in some cases or there is no known cause, but pain continues. This pain has become chronic and just became difficult to diagnose and treat.

HOW DO OPIOIDS ATTACH
TO PAIN RECEPTORS?

When we are in pain we have the option of taking opioids. Again, opioids attach to pain receptors in the brain, spinal cord, and GI tract, and can block the perception of pain by blocking pain transmissions from the body to the brain. Opioids have the ability to control pain, but also control reward and addictive behaviors. There are three opioid receptors: mu, delta, and kappa, all exhibiting a different biological effect on the body. Opioid receptors can be activated endogenously (from within), and exogenously (using medications), which simply means that your body produces natural painkillers, and medications are synthesized to act similar to your natural painkillers.

There are three categories of opioids, all of which attach to different receptors in the brain, they are: full agonists, partial agonists, and mixed agonists-antagonists. Full agonists, like morphine and fentanyl, continue increasing in efficacy over time and are the most effective at blocking pain. Partial agonists, like buprenorphine, are less effective and will eventually reach a ceiling of pain relief. Mixed agonists-antagonists, like pentazocine, only work on the mu-opioid receptor in the brain. Like partial agonists, these will also reach a ceiling in efficacy.

In some chronic pain conditions, like fibromyalgia, one theory is that there are less mu-opioid receptors available for unknown reasons, which translates into a reduction of pain relieving abilities, thereby reducing the analgesic effect, also reducing dependence behaviors. It is suggested that when you have less mu-opioid receptors, your reward/addiction properties are reduced or eliminated, even for non-opioid drugs that can be abused like marijuana, alcohol, and nicotine. And again, FM patients are suspected to have higher than normal levels of endogenous morphine, where adding drugs like Vicodin can increase pain. This may help explain how opioids do not work well for fibromyalgia sufferers for example. Additionally, the mu-opioid receptor is linked to depression when dependence is present. Like most medications, continuing to take opioids causes the body to adapt to the medication, resulting in dependence, and in rare cases—addiction. Over time, more of the drug is needed to achieve the same results. By default, opioids provide the feeling of euphoria by mediating the pleasure centers in the brain, along with blocking pain transmissions.

NEUROTRANSMITTERS AND FIBROMYALGIA
A SIMPLE EXPLANATION

There are dozens of neurotransmitters in humans, but for the purpose of understanding chronic pain, I intend to only focus on the most significant neurotransmitters: acetylcholine, dopamine, GABA, glutamate, melatonin, norepinephrine, serotonin, and substance P.

Biopsychology is one of a number of branches of psychology that deals with how neurotransmitters influence our behaviors, thoughts, and feelings (neuropsychology). Nerves are the starting point of pain and nerves are where you first receive impulses and where you start to process and transmit neurotransmitters.

At the end of the nerves are nociceptors, the receptors that detect pain, or actual or potential tissue damage. Nociceptors are everywhere, which explains why you can have pain everywhere with an illness like fibromyalgia. Nociceptors detect pain and transmit a signal to the brain, passing through the dorsal horn in your spine on the way to your brain, where it triggers the release of neurotransmitters, which activate other nerves that send the message to your brain (thalamus for processing), and sending out multiple pain messages.

Multiple pain messages help to explain how we experience several types of pain, and several levels of severity of pain. Everyone reacts differently, and how we react to pain is stored in our brain for future use, or reference to future pain—via perineuronal nets. In most cases, the older you get, and the more pain you have experienced in life, prepares you for future pain, building a tolerance to pain along the way (the brain remembers the pains you have experienced).

Thus pain becomes a normal part of life. What was just explained, describes *acute* pain that is said to serve a purpose. *Chronic* pain on the other hand, has no purpose. With chronic pain, the nerves being triggered become accustomed to being in pain, causing physiological changes to the affected nerves and surrounding areas, becoming chronic. In most cases, chronic pain is difficult or impossible to diagnose or pinpoint. With many chronic illnesses, like fibromyalgia, this is what happens and the nervous system becomes the source of the pain, making pain next to impossible to treat or manage.

NEUROTRANSMITTERS

The primary role of neurotransmitters (NTs) are to activate receptors, through an excitatory or inhibitory response, to affect mood, appetite, anxiety, sleep, aggression, temperature, heart rate, fear, and numerous other psychological and physical events. Excitatory NT's stimulate receptors, while inhibitory NT's block receptors (i.e. Vicodin inhibits pain receptors). Many actions can trigger the release of NT's. It is suggested that chronic stress, poor nutrition, and fast paced lives lead to the depletion of neurotransmitter levels. To some of you this sounds like your life before fibro arrived.

There are three primary types of NT's: amino acids, peptides, and monoamines. *Amino acids*: glycine, glutamate, aspartate, and GABA. *Monoamines*: acetylcholine, dopamine, norepinephrine, epinephrine, histamine, and serotonin. *Peptide*: substance P, endorphins, oxytocin, insulin, glucagon, vasopressin, and many more. NT's are made primarily from amino acids, which mostly come from your diet. It is suspected that neurons communicate via chemical release. Most effective psychoactive drugs (like antidepressants and narcotics) affect the neurotransmitters at one level or another, altering brain chemistry. All NT's are interconnected through a delicate system of balance. General anxiety disorder is suggested to be a result of the malfunction of several NT's in the brain, making GAD difficult to treat effectively.

Neurotransmitter's carry impulses between nerve cells, primarily dopamine, serotonin, and norepinephrine. Some foods are known to influence the brains behavior, and thus the neurotransmitters that regulate behavior. Serotonin is suggested to be released from carbohydrate foods, thus making junk foods—comfort foods. You eat these foods, serotonin is released, and tension is reduced.

Alternatively, if norepinephrine or dopamine were released (from proteins), you would feel excited or alert, versus relaxed, as with serotonin. Complex carbs and fatty acids (like salmon and white fish) would then stimulate the release of norepinephrine and dopamine. Foods high in saturated fats (like burgers and fries) will lead to slow thinking, and fatigue. Eating more carbs than protein relaxes you, while eating more protein than carbs alerts you. So fats inhibit the production of neurotransmitters. Eating simple carb foods provides a quick burst of energy, and then produces fatigue and depression shortly after.

Beyond these attributes, our body chemistry can also be affected by thoughts, emotions, and behaviors. Low levels of norepinephrine are observed in depressed people, for which relaxation can stimulate an increase of norepinephrine. Depression, anxiety, sleep issues, and sexual activity can be positively influenced by the release of endorphins, of which exercise can stimulate.

So clearly, all of our neurotransmitters can be affected by many different things, positively and negatively. When all of these things cannot be managed by you, you can turn to medications like antidepressants to help. Permitting yourself the positive influences and eliminating the negative ones (especially catastrophic thinking) in your life can essentially promote wellness. If you are able to do a number of the positive behaviors (exercise, nutrition, meditation, stress control, guided imagery, or talk therapy) that influence the production of serotonin, you will be able to manage pain and depression to some degree without medication.

Dramatic events in your life like a death, serious injury, or chronic illnesses have the ability to cause an increase in depression, however, most often only temporarily. Studies have concluded that over a period of time, neurotransmitter levels will return to normal when the stressful event has passed. This period of time can be up to a few years, depending on the event, the person's coping skills, support structure, and future ability to move on, etc. If the stressor continues, the depression can become chronic and difficult to manage without medication.

Chronic worrying can have a negative effect on neurotransmitters too. *Conceptual* worrying is normal constructive worrying, and is involved in reaching goals, etc., whereas *reactive* worrying has destructive results. When disease or illness is present, there is a disruption in the flow of neurotransmitters. Reuptake is the process of the neurotransmitter being picked up by the axon terminal that originally released it. This is a normal process, and is the common way the action of norepinephrine, dopamine, and serotonin are interrupted and stopped as seen in chronic illness or depression, etc. Reuptake removes the neurotransmitters from the synaptic cleft where they then will not bind to their respective receptor, and will not perform their job.

Acetylcholine is both an excitatory and inhibitory neurotransmitter. It was the first NT to be discovered in 1921. It is found in the CNS and the PNS. It is involved in muscle stimulation and REM sleep. Botox inhibits acetylcholine from aiding in muscle stimulation, causing a form of temporary paralysis. Acetylcholine is linked to Alzheimer's disease (loss of acetylcholine).

Dopamine is an inhibitory neurotransmitter made in the brain, and is similar to adrenaline, and has a role in the reward system, social anxiety, motor system, cognition, and endocrine system. Dopamine controls movement, emotional response, pleasure, pain, plays a role in addiction, and it causes excitability. Thus dopamine plays a role in mental and physical health. When dopamine transmitting neurons die, the result is Parkinson's disease (little to no dopamine). Medications like dopamine agonists (Requip or Mirapex) originally developed to treat Parkinson's disease activate dopamine receptors when dopamine is absent. Dopamine agonists can also treat restless leg syndrome (as often seen in fibro), which is believed to be caused by a shortage of dopamine in the brain, and depression, schizophrenia, and similar mental disorders. For example, in schizophrenia, it is suggested that there may be an over active dopamine system. Dopamine agonists can reduce dopamine activity.

Drugs of abuse stimulate dopamine receptors, which can lead to addiction. *Sensitization* can occur when one takes dopamine antagonists for a long time, increasing the number of dopamine receptors. The receptors become more sensitive to dopamine, resulting in sensitization. The opposite may occur when dopamine agonists constantly stimulate dopamine receptors, decreasing the number of receptors, and the remaining receptors become less sensitive to dopamine. This is desensitization, or tolerance, resulting in a need for more and more exposure.

Long-term over or under stimulation of the dopamine receptors results in sensitization or desensitization, however, both can occur immediately with the use of illicit drugs. The body tries to maintain constant homeostasis (equilibrium), even when foreign substances are introduced. Drugs like cocaine, heroin, alcohol, nicotine, and amphetamines increase dopamine levels, (feel good response). Schizophrenia involves increased amounts of dopamine, therefore those suffering from schizophrenia may benefit from medications that block dopamine like clozapine, or chlorpromazine. Too little dopamine can result in Parkinson's disease (lack of muscle control).

Endorphin (endogenous morphine) is an inhibitory neurotransmitter involved in pain reduction, stress, fear, rage, anxiety, and pleasure. It is structurally similar to common opioids like morphine (but not addictive); opioids attach to endorphin receptors. They are produced by the pituitary gland and the hypothalamus during certain events like exercise, pain, excitement, eating spicy foods, and sex. So eating a hot chili pepper can release endorphins.

Maintaining positive thoughts release endorphins (like the placebo effect). Being inspired can release endorphins through the pleasure response. Acupuncture can release endorphins, so can eating chocolate (the food drug). Also, being scared, laughing, and getting some sun can all release endorphins. Lacking endorphins can cause mental disorders like OCD and depression. For some, self-mutilation can release endorphins. If endorphins flood the hypothalamus or go on high alert, you can experience the fight-or-flight response, which is not healthy all the time—as seen in fibromyalgia. So when you have fibro, you want an increase of endorphins to make you feel better and the best way to get them is through exercise.

GABA (gamma aminobutyric acid) is an inhibitory neurotransmitter. Tranquilizers act to enhance GABA's effects. Low levels of GABA can lead to anxiety disorders. GABA can stop the excitatory neurotransmitter's that may cause anxiety. Alcohol and barbituates stimulate GABA receptors. Very low levels of GABA can lead to epilepsy. Anti-anxiety medications like benzodiazepines affect the GABA receptors. GABA and glutamate balance each other. Also, alcohol and GHB act on GABA, thus alcohol and GHB may reduce pain.

Glutamate is the major excitatory neurotransmitter in the brain and prevalent in the CNS. It is the most abundant NT in the brain, and is involved in learning and memory. Low levels of glutamate can result in sleepiness and reduced brain activity. Too much glutamate can result in neurodegenerative diseases like Alzheimer's, Parkinson's, Huntington's, Tourette's, and ALS, as well as leading to depression, OCD, and autism. Glutamate is one factor linked to fibrofog. A lumbar puncture (spinal tap) will show higher levels of glutamate and substance P in those with fibro.

Melatonin is a neurotransmitter produced by the pineal gland in the brain, and is secreted at night. Melatonin sends a signal to the body that it is time to sleep. The older one gets, the less melatonin is produced (especially over 40). Taking melatonin at bedtime can promote normal sleep patterns. It essentially helps to regulate the sleep cycle and our internal clocks naturally, among other things. When you have FM, you are likely not getting enough sleep, as well as having a disruptive sleep schedule (sleeping day and night). When this happens, you throw off your biological sleep clock and you can experience a number of FM type symptoms. Taking melatonin before bed can help to reset your clock. Since your immune system can be impacted with FM, taking melatonin can help to restore some immune function as well.

Norepinephrine (noradrenaline) is a neurotransmitter and hormone that helps to regulate mood, sleep, dreams, arousal, and the reward system. Like dopamine, it is a stimulant, fosters alertness, and aids in long-term memory and learning. In response to stress, as it acts as a hormone, and working with adrenaline (both released from the adrenal glands), it can increase blood pressure, constrict blood vessels and increase heart rate (fight-or-flight response).

As a neurotransmitter, norepinephrine transmits nerve impulses like other neurotransmitters. Antidepressants can inhibit the reuptake of norepinephrine (and serotonin). Too much norepinephrine can stimulate fear and anxiety—often seen in fibro. Stress can deplete adrenalin, and exercising can increase adrenalin. Sources for norepinephrine are almonds, apples, avocado, bananas, beef liver, blue-green algae, cheese, fish, grains, greens, lean meat, nuts, pineapple, poultry, and tofu.

Serotonin (5-HT; 5-hydroxytryptamine) is an inhibitory neurotransmitter that is involved in the transmission of nerve impulses. It is produced in the CNS and intestines. It helps regulate appetite, mood, emotions, memory, temperature, depression, muscle contraction, and sleep, and decreases nociception. It is manufactured in the brain using tryptophan. Tryptophan increases the amount of serotonin made by the brain. It is present in the CNS, hypothalamus, and basal ganglia. Low serotonin leads to depression, anxiety, apathy, fear, insomnia, fatigue, and addiction. Bananas and turkey contain proteins that help create serotonin.

Serotonin is suggested to be released from carbohydrate foods, thus making junk foods comfort foods (you eat these foods, serotonin is released, and tension is reduced). Serotonin begins being released under many circumstances, for example, making yourself comfortable with a warm shower. Reduced levels of serotonin can lead to depression, sleep issues, migraine, IBS, fibro, anger, OCD, carb cravings, and suicide. Antidepressants like Prozac act to prevent the reuptake of serotonin, leaving more of the NT directly in the synapse, allowing the medication to normalize the levels of serotonin. Prozac inhibits the reuptake of serotonin, leaving more serotonin in the synaptic gaps, allowing serotonin to perform its action, treating depression.

Substance P is responsible for pain transmissions to the periphery and CNS. It plays a major role in chronic pan conditions, asthma, psoriasis, IBD, migraine, schizophrenia, depression, and anxiety. Injured peripheral nerves cause the release of substance P into the spinal cord, transmitting pain messages. It is suggested that with fibromyalgia, substance P may be sent to the brain much more often than is necessary, resulting in pain with no etiology and wind-up type pain. Substance P is seen in levels three times higher in fibro sufferers, suggesting a higher degree of pain sensation. To date, nothing is approved to control levels of substance P.

Antidepressants do so much more than treat depression. The stigma that physicians have traditionally explained to fibro sufferers that their symptoms are *in their head* or psychosomatic begins to make some sense—when you consider the relationship between chronic fibro type pain, and the role of neurotransmitters. The relationship is strong and the overlap is significant. The next time your physician suggests antidepressants to treat your illness that IS NOT depression, consider that antidepressants help to alleviate pain, among many other symptoms, at higher doses.

There are three clinical types of pain associated with FM: hyperalgesia, allodynia, and paresthesia. Hyperalgesia is the term for pain amplification. FM sufferers have an unknown process whereby pain that would not be considered that significant in the average person is amplified in us. This is why sitting on a bleacher seat for an hour makes our butt and back extremely sore for days after, and a normal person walks bleacher—butt off in 10 minutes. The three FM drugs approved by the FDA target hyperalgesia (nih.gov).

Allodynia is the pain that comes from hypersensitivity all over your body from the lightest touches. Likely a neuropathic pain, it explains why your shirt hurts the hair on your arm as it rubs it, or how a massage would cause intolerable pain when others would find it relaxing. This pain originates from nociceptors, and comes in three forms: tactile, which is the pain you get from touching; mechanical, which is the pain of something moving across your skin; and thermal, which is the pain from hot or cold temperature (nih.gov). The pathophysiology of chronic pain as it relates to FM pain is that it has no underlying pathology so it is difficult to treat. This is why all we have today is a broad approach of interdisciplinary medicine, or a treatment team which combines every way known to man to provide some relief, but not significant for the general FM public.

CHRONIC PAIN AND PAIN STATES

Hyperalgesia and *allodynia* (pain states) are two common behavioral tests used in chronic pain studies, and typically major problems for pain patients. Hyperalgesia is the increased sensitivity to a noxious stimuli and allodynia is the increased sensitivity to a non-noxious stimuli.

With hyperalgesia, one would experience a minor response to noxious stimuli as pain to the hand from a pin prick, for example, which would be recognized as a baseline response. Most everyone would consider this to be painful. Hyperalgesia describes an increased sensitivity to stimuli that typically would not cause pain. Most people would say the pain would be a three on a 10-point scale, while someone who suffers from chronic pain and has hyperalgesia, (e.g., from fibromyalgia) would rate the pain as a six on a 10-point scale. Over time, individuals using opioids can develop opioid-induced hyperalgesia, which is a hypersensitivity to stimuli caused by the drugs. This can even develop into allodynia in severe cases.

With allodynia, one will experience a painful response to non-noxious stimuli. This means that an experience that is normally not painful to anyone will be painful to someone with allodynia. An example would be that someone with fibromyalgia experiences pain in their hair follicles as they put on a shirt and the material rub's along their hair. Allodynia is resistant to most medications, so treating this pain is often unsuccessful.

IDENTIFYING AND TREATING CHRONIC PAIN

The reporting figures for chronic pain vary greatly as a result of a non-standardized definition for the many different types of chronic pain, respectively. There may never be an acceptable definition for chronic pain disorders for this reason, and also because most often there is no identifiable cause. Chronic pain must be approached on a patient-needs basis, as no two individuals have congruent symptoms. Chronic pain sufferers' pain will vary based on individual differences, like personality, their capacity to cope with adversity or their resilience. This point reinforces the idea that the scientific model for disease cannot be accurately applied to chronic pain. Chronic illness has many possible influences or explanations for its presence. Treatment, therefore, should be adapted accordingly.

The way chronic pain is viewed may need to be reevaluated often. There are hidden attractors in understanding chronic pain; meaning regardless of what effort is put into resolution, no specific outcome will be evident. Chronic pain still eludes most clinicians overall. Embracing change with regard to chronic pain will continue to force improvements in treatment. Depending on the specifics of the chronic pain patient, the elements of treatment can be very broad to produce a positive outcome. Essentially, clinicians who propose to apply a complementary approach to the complexity of chronic pain stand to provide more opportunity for success in outcome.

One in four adults worldwide suffer from chronic pain, primarily musculoskeletal pain. It is the most common reason for absenteeism from work and disability. I believe we must address our fibro early, during the acute phase, before it becomes chronic. This involves identifying potential risk factors which is difficult to do. More importantly, a treatment program involves the patient willingly adopting self-management coping strategies for their pain. The difficulty involved in this part of the treatment is the patients *coping readiness level*, which will have a significant impact on the success of the pain management treatment. In order for this type of treatment to be effective, the patient must be open to changing behaviors, since much of the treatment focuses on encouraging them to take an active role in their pain management.

Often by the time a patient has reached a treatment phase that looks promising, a long time has passed and he has developed maladaptive coping strategies that are counterproductive to new treatment, and sometimes impossible to reverse. We develop bad habits out of a need to survive. Chronic pain becomes a rigid barrier to health. Much like the idea that fibromyalgia has traditionally been a phenomenon in the medical field, overlooked by many clinicians, and thus perpetuating the illness, chronic pain itself has become even more pandemic and is not being properly identified, addressed, and treated today.

Physicians need to better identify potential chronic pain indicators in the acute phase, where treatment is much more likely to be effective, before patients transition into the chronic phase. Pain assessment and intervention methods are more frequently being used in the treatment of chronic pain versus a traditional medical model approach. Today it is much more common practice to see patients undergo a multidisciplinary approach that involves the patient self-managing their condition to a large degree.

HOW WE VIEW PAIN TRANSLATES INTO HOW WE REACT TO PAIN

The patient and the physician do not typically view pain with the same perspective. The patient is in pain and wants relief, and therefore visits their physician with expectations of relief, or a cure. The physician, when confronted with chronic pain, especially fibromyalgia, as the main concern, is often left to assemble a puzzle looking for the source of the pain to treat, or eliminate. The problem with chronic pain is partly in the perspective and the terminology. Most of the time chronic pain cannot be cured or eliminated and physicians know this, but patients do not understand it. Some experts suggest that some medical terms should be changed for some chronic illnesses that would help to set and maintain the patient's perspective.

A change in the language that is commonly used by all clinicians and pharmaceutical companies, etc., could lead to a change in patient (societal) perspective and overall expectations. Patients would stop chasing a cure and look to the *management* of their chronic illness/pain, which would lead to a higher percentage of self-management success for patients. When the clinician fails to adequately identify symptoms, and further resulting psychological disorders, it is almost impossible for the clinician and the patient to work toward an integrative approach to wellness. I think it is the responsibility of the clinician to present such a therapeutic alliance to the patient, if they desire optimum results. Essentially, the patient and the clinician have to develop a management plan for care, especially in the face of chronic symptoms like pain, which are unlikely to be eliminated or cured. We need to change the way we, as patients, view, react, and accept our illness if we want to get beyond the suffering of it.

CHRONIC PAIN: CIRCULAR OR LINEAR CAUSE?

Some experts argue whether chronic pain has a linear or circular causation. Linear causality dictates that "A causes B," and in the case of acute pain, this is almost always certainly the case. However, in chronic pain, there are flaws in using the linear model, and chronic pain is often perceived as being circular. The clinician attempts to interrupt the cycle since curing the cause of the pain is not always plausible. A clinician who assumes to treat chronic pain using the linear model stands to misdirect treatment, causing delays in pain relief and increased suffering for their patient. Inappropriately addressing chronic pain early on only exacerbates symptoms, and often leads to psychological disorders like depression—further reducing the pain threshold. This is precisely where the physician's focus on the physical symptoms alone may leave the mental component unaddressed; and thus adding to the viciousness of the cycle of pain.

THE COST OF CHRONIC PAIN

Often chronic pain sufferers will ignore the psychological component of pain out of fear or misinformation. Chronic pain affects the amount and quality of sleep we achieve. As a result, it can become more difficult to fall asleep and stay asleep, which leads to or exacerbates pain, depression, fatigue, and memory problems. Chronic pain effects over 76 million people in the United States alone more than diabetes (21 million), heart disease and stroke (19 million), and cancer (1.5 million) combined. Roughly 50 million people in the United States currently have a diagnosis of arthritis, rheumatism, gout, lupus, or fibro. The total cost of healthcare due to chronic pain is roughly $300 billion and another $315 billion in the United States annually, which include the cost for healthcare, the cost of lost income, and the cost of lost productivity (CDC, 2010; NCHS, 2010). When depression sets in as a result of chronic pain, we begin to feel hopeless, and become more angry, moody, and easily frustrated. Anxiety can exacerbate pain, by the increase in muscle tension or spasms. If you suffer from depression, anxiety, or other psychological disorders and do not address your issues with counseling, your chronic pain will become worse.

PAIN MANAGEMENT

Less than 50 percent of chronic pain sufferers achieve relief from even the most powerful of pain relievers, and that reduction in pain only reaches 30—40 percent. Chronic pain patients, on average, seek treatment for seven years. The experience, maintenance, and exacerbation of pain are greatly influenced by psychosocial and behavioral factors; therefore, *self-management* becomes one of the most important steps in recovery for the patient. The patient has to become their own advocate and begin to manage their wellness.

There are a few self-management approaches that have shown to improve the lives of chronic pain patients like insight-oriented therapies, operant conditioning, and cognitive behavioral therapy. *Insight-oriented* approaches focus on somatic presentations of early relationship experiences. These may impact the onset and maintenance of chronic pain. Focusing on these may improve emotional regulation. *Operant conditioning* focuses on reducing pain behaviors down to extinction. Patients are encouraged to take a large part in the personal management of their therapy to reach their goals. *Cognitive behavioral therapy* is designed to improve function overall. The self-management process may involve some or all of the following: proper nutrition, exercise, stress management, problem solving, goal setting, pacing of activities, assertiveness, biofeedback, relaxation, meditation, guided imagery, and hypnosis. These modalities can be used to teach the patient self-control or management and hopefulness. These three treatment interventions among others actually teach you how to reduce pain and other symptoms to a tolerable level. This is a real pain reduction you won't achieve with pills and has helped tens of thousands of people with chronic pain conditions. Will it make you pain free? Absolutely not. Will it be easy? Absolutely not. But take my word for it, you can't afford not to add one or more of these interventions to your wellness tool box.

Chronic pain is a self-limiting condition. The impact can be significant on the individual, but also on society, when one considers the cost of health care, productivity, and personal suffering. Most often pain is viewed as a medical issue with objective evidence to support it. The rest of the time, pain falls into the category of psychological or somatic, in the absence of objective evidence. Many patients can have their symptoms or illnesses overlooked if their condition lies *between* a psychological or physical diagnosis. Patients can become very difficult to treat as a result.

THE EPIDEMIOLOGY OF CHRONIC PAIN

There is a strong relationship between chronic pain and psychological comorbidity. By definition, pain can clearly be experienced with or without physical trauma. Pain can be classified as a general medical condition or as a pain disorder. If pain is classified as a general medical condition, the medical condition will be to blame for the trauma or severity of the pain. If the pain is severe enough to cause psychological factors along with physical factors, and cannot be explained by another condition, it may be classified as a somatoform disorder. Additionally, pain meets the criteria of chronic after it has continued for three months, doesn't end as expected, and doesn't respond to most treatments.

Chronic pain can be comorbid with psychiatric conditions as chronic pain increases the risk for psychiatric conditions, as well as psychiatric conditions increase the risk for chronic pain. Both chronic pain and psychiatric conditions can affect prognosis and treatments. The patient likely needs to address both of the above simultaneously to be treated as a whole and not miss something. Treating one piece of this puzzle and not the rest will not be an effective solution to the problem as a whole.

CHRONIC PAIN: GET CONTROL OF IT

All of us know what pain is, but none of us know when it may strike or when it may leave, and one in four of us have chronic pain. That makes chronic pain more prevalent, misdiagnosed, misunderstood, and mistreated than any one major illness. Pain is capable of producing pathological changes in the brain and spinal cord, and that effect can be devastating.

Acute pain is a universal phenomenon the world over. But chronic pain is not so simple. The concept of pain is still so far from being understood in mainstream medicine, and that is why it is so important that we understand as much as we can about the psychology of our illness, so that we may manage it. When you have chronic pain, you lie somewhere in the middle of the spectrum that explains pain from conception to cure.

If these is one thing that you can do today, it's to change your perspective of the world. You can view the obstacles of pain and fatigue as illusions and overcome them. Tomorrow is going to come whether you are ready for it or not so why not at least equip your attitude for what lies ahead.

"Things turn out best for people who make the best of the way things turn out."

—John Wooden

"One of the secrets of life is making stepping stones out of stumbling blocks."

—Jack Penn

This is true with disease. What we get really does depend on what we are looking for. Everything matters, and our attitude and spirit are everything when we lose grasp of our health. Wellness is right in front of us; it is in books and on the Internet and we have to be willing to act on the impulses to make ourselves well again.

The prognosis of chronic pain is not exciting. Pain leads to more pain. In FM chronic pain leads to additional pain and symptoms, and can even lead to depression and anxiety among other things. These comorbid symptoms are what perpetuate our primary illness and wreak havoc on our body systems overall. Severe pain exacerbates other issues and can even cause cardiac issues which is why it is so important to manage your pain. Easier said than done though, since you may have tried every intervention and drug known to man, and still have no significant relief. The trick is to keep moving forward and advocating for yourself because no one else will do it for you. The idea here is for me to reduce some of the time it takes to eliminate what works and does not work.

If you are suffering from depression it is important to control this as well since depression exacerbates pain—another vicious cycle of FM. Since chronic pain can lower your self-esteem, you will want to surround yourself with the right kind of environment to remain mindful of your mission to feel better. You do not want to catastrophize about your situation. It is also suggested that chronic pain perpetuates fibrofog, cognition, attentiveness, memory, verbal ability, and concentration.

When your physician or disability representative asks you to describe your pain or fatigue or whatever on a one to 10-point scale, it is difficult. As a rule, zero would mean pain free, and 10 would be, well, what is 10? I've been asked this question 50 times and always struggle with it because rating the way you feel in response to a chronic symptom is not like scoring a talent show. It is more of a sliding scale of ability or disability; of can and cannot; of used to and can no longer do.

If pain does not get you, fatigue will, and if your bladder lets up, your diarrhea flares up! Rarely could I say, my pain is an eight today and have the person asking me understand what it means, exactly. This is another FM-ism that we are stuck with and have to make due with. More commonly my answer to that question would be something like this "well the pain is so significant, I cannot find a comfortable position and I am having throbbing pain in eight different muscle groups. My fatigue is so overwhelming, I cannot be away from a horizontal position for more than 20 minutes, and a flight of stairs makes me exhausted and my whole body shake for a half hour. My headache is to the degree that I cannot even focus in one spot long enough to have a conversation, and today is day 58—30 of which have been a migraine. And this is the third shirt I have put on today, because I have soaked the other two with sweat from NO activity." So go ahead and rate that accordingly!

CHALLENGES AND BARRIERS TO CHRONIC PAIN

The topic of chronic pain and psychological comorbidity is one of growing concern in the medical field. There seems to have been a paradigm shift from physicians blaming chronic pain on trauma or injury (or depression), to recognizing chronic pain as its own disease, capable of being comorbid with numerous other conditions and syndromes, both physical and psychological (biopsychosocial).

Medicine has moved from a pharmacologically based treatment approach for chronic pain, to a multidisciplinary, complementary approach, often involving very little if any pharmaceuticals. Many physicians also share the belief that managing chronic illness and its comorbidity is often more appropriate and reasonable than curing the illness. Much of the management of the chronic condition is left to the patient, since the clinician can only do so much for the patient, and medicine will only go so far. Creating a true partnership between the patient and all clinicians will prove most beneficial in the long-run.

There are some additional barriers that present challenges for physicians treating chronic illness. There is sometimes a lack of understanding opioids and their efficacy or spectrum. There also seems to be a negative stigma about prescribing opioids in general, as physicians fear creating addicted patients.

There also exist barriers that are brought on by the patient. Poor communication can be a critical miss in the doctor's office. A patient needs to be able to effectively explain their condition to their physician. The patient may not properly participate in the treatment for the fear of side effects or addiction to medications.

Clinicians need to explain the value of drugs and interventions while minimizing the risks—where possible. The fear of pain itself poses a strong barrier that exacerbates pain. Beyond the physician and patient, the health care system in general can be a major constraint to treatment.

POSITIVE ACTIONS
WITH FIBROMYALGIA

You have to find a coping mechanism to reverse your fibro, and your best bet is to have several. Your wellness plan should be extremely well rounded with multiple layers of positive actions and with hope around every corner. You have to slow down your thinking just long enough to retrain yourself because negative thoughts can become actions and soon you could be thinking and doing actions that are counterproductive to your recovery. Discover your strengths. Focus on what your strengths are and they will carry you through to your next successful moments. Eliminate self-defeating thoughts, ideas, and behaviors.

Don't schedule downtime into your day. If you do you will take it and it becomes a slippery slope. Suddenly you are relaxing 10 hours a day and living a counterproductive lifestyle. Instead, schedule in activities for the whole day and you will begin to establish habits that follow the normal human desire to accomplish things promoting forward movement versus stagnation. Don't get upset if you fall behind or don't get everything done because you are trying to build in new positive habits that will sustain you in your weakest moments where you would have otherwise given up in the past. This will take time so don't allow mini failures to become real setbacks. Research suggests that those who work the hardest in work worth doing live the longest. Every day I work as hard as I can short of causing setbacks. This is because I have created a wellness plan that involves meaningful activities that promote quality of life. This translates into a longer, better life, even with chronic illness.

Save some words of wisdom or comfort that you find particularly hopeful. These words can sustain you through the long nights when you feel the challenges of your illness at its worst. Remember your thoughts can turn into your actions. You become what you think about so positive thinking makes you positive. I know the faster you come to grips with your reality and begin accepting it, the faster you can begin to overcome or reverse your illness, one truth at a time. You have to be truthful to yourself to move forward or else you will be at a standstill.

It is ironic how often little things in life like music can change the tone of your mood. You can completely transform your attitude with the right setting, and music can guide that tone. FM is considered to be one of the most common chronic illnesses in the United States today. Until there are doctors with a more thorough ability to diagnose and a standard of treatment in comprehensive medicine there will remain a great struggle for sufferers.

The good news is that history has shown that many illnesses that are taken deadly serious today were not taken serious at some point in the infancy stages of research, and this is hopeful for FM. Several illnesses used to puzzle physicians at one time, but are accepted as mainstream diseases today—and fibro research is exploding.

The best medicine is a positive attitude, a strong hope, and doing what you are passionate about. Find activities that you love or that compliment your positive traits and you will reap the benefits and simple pleasures. Find something that is rewarding and work towards a goal that is important, and your attitude will remain positive. Living with and without limitations can be defining for most of us and can provide a baseline of understanding. In the end, what really matters is what you need to start doing now.

At some point you may work up to a low dose maintenance drug schedule which becomes a part of your lifestyle, once your FM is under control of course. It is very important for you to keep an open mind. Your determination, attitude, and knowledge about your illness are at the core of your wellness. You will find that happiness is a strong medicine as well. It can be very difficult to observe and then change behaviors and habits that may not seem obvious to you, but that will cause flares. Pursuing cognitive behavioral therapy can help you function through the symptoms. It can also help you to eliminate your negative actions, behaviors, and attitudes to learn how to turn negative into positive, and learn to control your energy and decrease pain and sleep better—overall improving your mental picture.

Do not compare yourself now, to who you used to be. You may never be that exact person again. You will have to move past that grieving process and loss of self to accepting who you are today. You cannot spend too much time hoping for improvement to that old level because you will constantly be let down. Focus your hope on your new expectations of who you are in realistic terms and I promise you will come to terms with that and it will be one more step that you will not fall backwards from.

I like the idea of creating a *positive effort list* of positive actions that we can do to add to our recovery and wellness plan. Research suggests that you need to make every effort to improve every aspect of your life to aid in your recovery—the key here is self-improvement. I take inspiration from anywhere I can get it. You will discover that keeping a symptom diary can be helpful to you to look at trends in your symptoms as they relate to your lifestyle; it can be an eye opening experience. Plus it will serve as a great record as you document your progress for you, your physician, and possibly your disability provider.

It can also be motivating to write since you may feel better as you read what you wrote in the past as you progress in your treatment. Keeping track of your life through journaling may become a lifelong requirement to set boundaries and to keep your illness in check, avoiding bad habits, and shaping positive behaviors. Keep in mind, almost anything in your life could potentially be a trigger for flares.

WHY IS IT SO IMPORTANT TO FIGHT AND KEEP ON FIGHTING?

Perpetuation factors like chronic pain make everything harder, including recovery. Your willingness to get well is not nearly enough. You have to make a commitment to your recovery action plan and hold firm to it. You may often feel defeated, and if your symptoms are as bad as mine are, you have to be willing to start, have the courage to move forward and the faith to finish—day after day.

Make the future you are constructing better than the past you are dreaming of. Positive messages ring out like a symphony, and can be very powerful. You have to develop a new focus on wellness and never focus on what you fear. There is a fear that accompanies chronic illness but I fear the unknown much more. What you are doing right now by educating yourself is staying ahead of the fear, and in control of your life.

You need to learn how to be motivated and inspired. I became motivated by pain and inspired by hope. Positive people see setbacks as opportunities to grow. As in anything you do in your life that matters, you live and learn, and you learn from mistakes and setbacks. The road to wellness can be long and twisty and most likely you will get lost a few times, and that can set you back. Finding your way through *education* becomes an opportunity to grow. You need to relearn how to live a life of abundance again. I used to live with abundance. Now I live with less. Fighting a chronic illness has a way of simplifying things. Not only do you learn to do less, you may only do what is truly important, and you may find a way to refine your whole world, partly because the need to reduce stress can force a downsizing. You may also find that your time is precious and stop wasting it on unimportant things like I did.

You may be dealing with financial constraints too, family/ marriage pressures, work issues, or SS and disability. By the time you get to this point your abilities and resources are maxed out and you may have to make desperate moves. This is why lifestyle modifications can be so beneficial. Expecting the flare-ups and educating yourself and preparing for negative outcomes will lessen the impact when setbacks strike. We need to find the balance between ability and disability. Figure out what you can and cannot do. Then figure out what has to be done, and then put it into action. Clearly there are going to be physical limitations you will notice, or you have to assess; stay busy doing what matters, and make time for downtime absent from everything. Focus on what you can do, not what you cannot do. Make a written list of do's and don'ts and be true to yourself. Consider the statement, "If you don't use it, you lose it," and find a happy medium.

Keep in mind that greater disability is a slippery slope. Fight and keep fighting in spirit, not always in action. Your mind has healing capabilities, but it also has damaging ones. Part of your road to recovery is thinking yourself well. This goes for any illness or injury. We need to retrain our bodies to work correctly. If you have advanced symptoms your body may not always do what you want it to. The loss of faculties can lead to toxic pessimism. Expect that you will face losses. Some loss is acceptable, and it could always be worse. When you commit to a wellness approach, you will learn to assign limits to yourself, but you will also be able to retrain yourself to meet your changing needs. This is a big adjustment and takes considerable effort. It does not happen overnight. This takes an interdisciplinary approach and a positive attitude.

We of course have to work with our doctors, our medical support staff, our chiropractors, our masseuses, our acupunctural therapists, our therapists, our families, and our state disability and so on. This team approach will add to our success. Our bodies lack the key function of restoration and we need to get it back. For most, it starts with poor sleep. We miss out on the stage three and four sleep we need and get shorted the critical restoration function. Then it is believed that we have ATP and mitochondrial dysfunction which further affects our restorative function. Then the lack of exercise becomes a perpetuating factor. Again this illness quickly becomes a slippery slope so maintaining a positive attitude is critical. Think yourself well and you will see benefits.

Self-control becomes another function that will keep us in the driver seat. It seems like we lose control of some of the basic faculties as the illness advances over time. Maintaining control over specific attributes of your recovery plan that matter like, diet, fitness, your activities, and especially your outlook will be an advantage. You stand to benefit in numerous ways by maintaining your weight. Face it—the less you have to carry around, the better you will feel.

First we must take ownership of our illness or we are just spinning our wheels. Finding a support structure of some kind can help give you strength when you need it most. We need to become more self-aware of who we are and what we are capable of doing. We need to control and appropriately limit our activity and forward moving processes in our minds. This will aid in maintaining control overall. What we thought we were capable of doing, and what we think we can deliver, contributes to failure and causes setbacks, if our expectations are set too high. Set realistic parameters for yourself.

We need to learn to calm the soul. There's more to relaxation than sitting comfortably or lying down. You should create an environment that fosters *total relaxation*, for those periods of down time. Placing consideration on sound, lighting, and distractions like TV, phone, and computers can only add to your relaxation.

We have to arrive at a place where we can let go of some of our pain and stress and so on. Painkillers will only do part of the job for a percentage of the population. Once you gain emotional control you will see benefits. We must control our mood and especially our temper. I think it is easy to get mad when you face defeat and especially when you face it accompanied by chronic symptoms. Not to mention some days it seems like everything has gone wrong.

Again, many of us are our own practitioners and part of our medicine is constant self-control. Proper diet means more than most other efforts. You are what you eat and that goes double with FM. Exercise falls into a needed but somewhat subjective category. When we are healthy it is hard to get to the gym or go jogging much less when life throws up other obstacles. It takes an even stronger commitment when you feel sick most of the time. But, we need to exercise to avoid deconditioning.

We may continue to experience myriad obstacles as our illness progresses but we must maintain focus and face those challenges point by point. It is a good idea to maintain some kind of movement. That being said, figure out each day what level of fitness you can tolerate. Keeping moving will help with stiffness and deconditioning, etc.

You cannot climb a smooth mountain. There may be unbelievable challenges. Many of us will not make it all the way to the top. But the good news is there is plenty of room along the way for those who fall down, or who pitch their tents for a short stay, or for those who just cannot go any further…today. I have learned to accept who I am, today, and so can you. You may not ever fully get your life back as it once was, and you may never be able to do all of the things you love. This may become your new reality and until you can embrace it, you are likely to keep facing setbacks.

HOW DO YOU CATEGORIZE YOUR SYMPTOMS?

Essentially the lack of sleep may be in the top three most undesirable symptoms of FM. That being said, at night we are fighting an uphill battle between insomnia and exhaustion, to bladder dysfunction, to pain, anxiety, and even depression. We must assign goals and deadlines and live by them. We have to meet these goals hourly, daily and weekly. These tools, techniques, and skills are not really optional and success will be definable by how well we champion each and every challenge, and it all starts with the right attitude.

I find that doctor's orders are much easier to follow *to the letter*, especially when it is serious. This is no different. Everything we're talking about here has to be absorbed fast, properly digested, and made into a program, because programs are easier to memorize, get comfortable with, and follow long-term. Like diets, most people have more luck with a well-defined diet program that has requirements, guidelines, is measurable, and prohibits or encourages specific behaviors. This simplifies our routine, and simplicity fosters positive behavioral changes, and practicing those behaviors forces habits and habit forming changes lives. My daily goal is essentially the same as my long-term goal—to increase function, decrease symptoms, and get back to a normal life. By definition our quality of life is not that poor. There are much sicker people out there and it could always be worse.

I think we can all do this on our own, meaning we all possess the inner strength to achieve success. There are going to be times when we have to rely on the assistance from others, especially in the health care field and it is very helpful to find *fibro-friendly* practitioners of any kind regardless of subspecialty. We are all going to have to perform at our best at home because those who *HAVE* to live with us are suffering almost as much as us. They are required to observe our illness in all its forms and furthermore pick up all the pieces along the way. We have to maintain a delicate balance between the good and the bad and how much we are able to conceal and tolerate, without *burning out* our families. Since everything in life becomes harder on us, think what it does to our families.

We have to learn who we are and what we are capable of from one minute to the next. You will have more success if you understand your illness, take an aggressive approach to wellness, and stay on course with nutritional principles. As an educated patient, you will have a stronger focus and will be more likely to remain compliant with your program. We must maintain an awareness of our body as we begin to condition it toward health. Each movement or function must be done in accordance with our limitations at that time and that is tough to gauge. Since there are often no patterns or similarities in our symptoms, we have to manufacture the kind of environment that fosters family values—not just misery.

Bold moves like the Governor of Michigan, Jennifer Granholm, creating a *Fibromyalgia Awareness Day* (5-12-09) are helpful to the cause. Removing the phrase, "My fibromyalgia is real" from advertisements and product campaigns and replacing it with a more relaxed approach to FM symptoms will also be beneficial, especially for the nonbelievers to see.

EMOTIONAL SUPPORT

So what do you tell friends when they ask about your health? I did not always have a great answer for this question. It always seemed like I could not deliver an accurate answer without prefacing them with some background information first. I felt like I could never tell someone immediately that I have fibromyalgia and have them understand; and to be honest, I was always embarrassed about the diagnosis. I figured whoever heard me say I had fibromyalgia would just think I was depressed or lazy or had emotional problems, and choose to avoid me afterwards— and truth be told, I did lose friends because of my inability to effectively deal with fibro early on. Or maybe they would picture that woman from the fibro drug commercials staring out a window on a sad, rainy day, and she looks as if she is one thought away from falling completely into a deep everlasting depression. Let's face it, public opinion is what it is for a reason, and it is not always easy explaining it.

Or then there are the commercials on TV and the radio or in magazines that start off with, "my fibromyalgia is real," as if this provides validation to the public. In my experience with this strenuous movement to validate the illness or provide public confidence, all it does is further push fibromyalgia into the fraud category and depression related. I realize that may sound like a counter-productive mentality, but the world can be cruel about stereotypes, and most of the time they hold no merit, but try explaining yourself out of that one to your friends when you are not working and you physically look fine.

Emotional support is important and many people are not getting it from their family and friends, much less from the public and the medical community. It is not uncommon to be doubted by everyone around you when you have FM, mostly because you do not look sick and you do not have a *valid* disease to explain to people why you are sick. So here is the answer to this problem. Education is the only way you will gain support from the nonbelievers. The more you know the better you will be able to explain what is happening with you, from an educated perspective, backed with facts and statistics that are hard to dispute. Nothing is quite as convincing as a solid argument. Then you ask those closest to you to read this or other books on fibro so they can better understand what you are going through.

While you are educating yourself you need to build the right medical support staff that will advocate for FM and *that* will relieve about half of your stress immediately. This is a big deal finding a doctor who will validate your illness and listen to your concerns. Remember that most physicians do not allow much more than 15 minutes for an average visit, so be wise in only asking the necessary questions during your time with him. Do your research first and ask what you cannot figure out on your own. This commitment from you also will show your doctor that you take your wellness very seriously and advocate for yourself to a high degree.

Before you know it you will feel comfortable in knowing as much as you can about this illness and this will allow time for you to breathe again. Once this happens you will slowly eliminate stress and that is when you will see the symptoms begin to reduce and eliminate. I am sure you will see symptom relief but I am also fairly sure you will not be symptom free until science finds a more effective way to alleviate symptoms or a cure. I am not asking for a cure today. I will settle for symptom relief for now and I will accept that it is up to me to get there. Can you accept that?

EVERYTHING MATTERS

Getting back to basics with a chronic illness like fibromyalgia requires lifestyle management. As patients, we must go beyond what physicians and pharmacists can do for us, and learn to live an abundant life *with* disease. Getting back to basics is really about doing everything you can on your own, before you put your faith in the hands of clinicians for symptom relief or a cure. Clinicians can only do so much, and in the case of most chronic illnesses, clinicians' hands are often tied.

Doing what we can means eating right, exercising for cardiovascular health and to avoid deconditioning, and wrapping your arms around your condition and managing it like your life depended on it. While I do feel that it takes a number of things to get you to wellness, getting back to basics will deliver you to a much higher degree of *treatable* for your clinicians. You are essentially handing yourself over to your clinicians and saying, "here you go, I have done what I can to allow my body to heal itself…I have purified my diet and maintained proper nutrition and avoided trigger foods and unhealthy foods. I have adopted an exercise curriculum and have stuck to it for many months. I have learned what I can about my illness and have committed to doing everything I can that moves me in the direction of getting well…now can you help me continue my approach toward wellness by taking this well-tuned specimen I am delivering you and help me move forward?"

This may sound unusual, but today many physicians are only *tolerant* to many chronic illnesses, knowing that they can only deliver you to a degree of symptom relief; and the rest is up to the patient, who is usually *not* doing the basics to survive.

If you present to your physicians like this, they will have no choice but to take you deadly serious as someone who is 100 percent dedicated to wellness, and they will be more likely to partner with you toward wellness. They will observe your commitment to getting better and will feel that much better that they are working with a strong candidate for improvement, versus someone who is looking for answers in the form of a pill, and who is unwilling to help themselves.

This is where we must step in and do what we can, on our own, and there are a few principles that may make all the difference between illness and wellness. So consider what kind of patient you are and what kind of patients are those who DO find symptom relief or become well, even if it is not a cure.

The concept of pain is still so far from being understood in mainstream medicine, and that is why it is so important that we understand as much as we can about the psychology of our illness, so that we may manage it to some degree.

Wake up every day and challenge yourself to attain everything you want to. Begin a routine of positive, productive activities. ONLY take steps in positive directions, and live your life as if nothing was wrong. Do not let your illness paralyze you. Finding hope is your responsibility, no one can do it for you. Fill your toolbox with the right kind of coping strategies so you will be equipped to face the challenges when they present. Control your environment. This helps to not fuel the fire. Slow down. Listen to relaxing music. My friend Mary Kay Foley helped me create some tools for wellness below. Observe the following:

How to have a good clinician visit

1. Schedule the appointment for in the a.m. to reduce anticipatory stress

2. Bring all medical and insurance cards, pharmacy number and fax

3. Determine if tests are to be done in case fasting blood work is needed

4. Take a friend or relative if you are not feeling well

5. Write down your top three most important issues/questions

6. Ask for script refills early in the visit or hand him a written list

7. Bring all medication bottles if it is a new doctor

8. If a new drug is prescribed, ask the purpose, effects, side effects

9. Ask doctor what criteria is for calling him with problems

10. Ask for name of nurse that handles the physician's patients

11. Ask any unanswered questions

12. Document everything (or record visit and transcribe notes later for your records)

Make a list of hope generators

1. Children

2. Spouse

3. Pets

4. Friends

5. Hobbies

6. Advocacy

7. Volunteering

8. Support group meetings

9. Exercising

10. Vacations

Fill your coping strategy toolbox

1. Tools for relaxation like meditation, music, tapes, videos, elimination of stressors

2. Assemble a box of favorite songs on CD's for easy access (or on IPOD)

3. Assemble a box of favorite videos that make you feel good or grateful or laugh

4. List of a half a dozen friends that you can call anytime. Or one or two if needed

5. When you have a pity party, do it well. Make a list of strengths and weaknesses

Learn how to not be a victim

1. Empower yourself against your own insecurities. If you tend to doubt yourself consistently, you need to build a sense of strength and confidence in yourself. Question your own inner critic and make a consistent effort to combat any negative thoughts that prevent you from moving forward. Realize that most of your inner criticism is flawed and that you are bringing yourself down by allowing yourself to think negatively.

2. Empower yourself physically. Feeling physically strong is part of feeling empowered. Address any medical issues you have been procrastinating about. Make that doctor's or dentist's appointment. Set up an exercise schedule. Take some self-defense or martial arts classes in order to gain confidence in yourself.

3. Empower yourself by being assertive. Gain power in your own situation by speaking up for yourself and others around you. There is no reason to be passive or to take things sitting down. Start with small steps. Work on

asking for what you want and clearly stating what your boundaries are in everyday situations. If someone takes you for granted or treats you poorly, either choose to walk away or choose to clearly express your disapproval. Value yourself enough to stand up for yourself. Realize that you do have power in stressful situations.

4. Empower yourself by setting and achieving goals. Giving up on yourself can be completely disempowering. If you have stopped setting and achieving goals to move you forward in a positive direction then you need to start again. Set small goals that will provide you with a sense of self-worth and pride in yourself. The more you realize that you are capable and competent in your own life, the more empowered you will feel.

5. Empower yourself by learning how to deal with anger and frustration. Work on your ability to handle anger and frustration by being proactive in a given situation. Realize that if you do not like a given situation you need to do something positive to change it. Confront any anxieties and fears by taking small steps to challenge yourself. If you have issues with controlling anger, get some coaching or counseling to get through it. Anger has the potential to hold you back and prevent you from thinking clearly.

6. Empower yourself by dealing with any emotional voids. If you feel lonely or disenchanted or bored frequently, you need to find things that will make you passionate and excited about life. Involve yourself in new activities where you can expand your social structure and look forward to different things throughout the week. If you have stopped reading, listening to music or working on hobbies you used to enjoy, get back into it. If you love animals, volunteer at an animal shelter or get a new pet. Get back into living life with joy and gain empowerment in the process.

FINDING HOPE WHERE
THERE IS NONE

I once had the opportunity to talk to a soldier that was wounded from a blast during wartime. He described the moment he knew something had happened, through when he thought he would be ok.

As I listened to every detail, I could not help but think of how his story was similar to my story, or at least his thoughts and physical actions toward the event were categorically similar to mine when my FM is at its worst. And that in many ways was similar to my story, at least in the simple details as they relate to hope and wishing and begging and praying and regret and loss. I realize that his story and the events he experienced were much more significant compared to mine, but it was just a story I related to when I was looking for hope. It inspired me to push on.

He lied there in the rain, too tired to move much, confused about his exact state, and focused heavily on pain. He felt severe pain radiating from all over his body. He could not really place the pain's location; just that it was more than he could bear and that was the best way to describe it. He tried to move but was surprised to realize that he hurt almost everywhere as he tried; no matter what part of his body he tried to move. Not much worked; even though his brain told his body to act.

All at one time he was so tired he wanted to sleep, but his heart was racing, his ears were ringing, and his vision was blurry. He was so thirsty and his mouth was so dry, he could not speak, but he knew what he wanted to say. His brain was foggy and his memory was patchy. By this time only seconds had passed since he had realized that something was not right. He knew he was in trouble, but he did not think anyone else realized, which filled him with fear. He wondered what others thought of him at that moment. He felt close to death, as he wished he could be close to God.

Thoughts began to race through his head about everything bad he had ever done; then everything wonderful he had ever done. He focused on his family and closed his eyes; needing a moment of hope in a moment of hopelessness. Pleading with himself; begging God to just be somewhere else; to just have another chance. Choking to swallow; pain increasing; fear filling up as hopelessness rises up in the four corners of his brain. Wishing he could sleep but his mind racing too fast to sleep; too much pain and too much stress, too much fear to sleep.

The next moment awakening in a hospital, stable and out of surgery; speechless with happiness; thinking about his ordeal; realizing what had occurred; not sure if he was going to be normal again; going to walk again; going to be the same again; alive; and filled with hope!

CONCLUSION

Fibro is suspected to impact the whole body, but specifically the endocrine system, the immune system, the sympathetic nervous system, the parasympathetic nervous system, the fine motor system, and the pain control systems are impacted most often and most significantly. These systems that are supposed to protect you malfunction. The sympathetic nervous system begins to malfunction causing an increase in the frequency and severity of the fight-or-flight response-releasing more adrenaline, causing fatigue and hypersensitivity. The fine motor system malfunctions affecting your muscles-beginning with shutting down some muscles, and overworking other muscles causing an increase in muscle pain. The endocrine system increases the production of cortisol which promotes soreness in tissues, extra tiredness, fatigue, hypersensitivity, and promotes deconditioning through inactivity. The parasympathetic nervous system begins to malfunction and prohibits restorative sleep and healthy digestive function. It also inhibits natural tissue healing by slowing the process down. The immune system malfunctions causing slow healing, fatigue, and hypersensitivity. Suddenly you realize that you don't just have pain and fatigue, you have mood swings, weight gain, cognition and memory issues, sleep issues, bowel and bladder issues, depression begins to settle in, and you feel that you cannot go on.

The visible system that is doing all the defending typically becomes the diagnosis. In other words, depending on which one of these systems is acting up the most, or presenting the most obvious group of symptoms will likely be the diagnosis your physician passes out to you, which is partly why fibro can be so hard to diagnose for some physicians. For example, if your nervous system seems to be the most in charge of your symptoms, you are likely to receive a diagnosis of fibro. If your endocrine system is dominant your physician is more likely to look at chronic fatigue syndrome. Different doctor = different diagnosis. Or maybe you had a complex case and it took several years to get a diagnosis? Again, these inferences are based on what limited understanding physicians have about putting this complex puzzle together. AND, since you likely have a number of symptoms that do not necessarily go together, you may receive multiple diagnoses-or no diagnosis.

We have a prototypical central pain syndrome causing a dysfunction in central pain processing. Fibromyalgia is a biopsychosocial illness that results in neurobiologic symptoms and our pain is multifocal not peripheral. Our genes predispose us to fibro, but our lifestyle or our environment triggers fibro. Stress exacerbates our symptoms. We have several neurotransmitters out of whack, triggering or exacerbating symptoms of fibro. We present with a decreased gray matter in the brain. Our pain volume is turned up in brain sensory processing, so our brain and spinal cord process pain incorrectly. Our brains are malleable (changeable) and neuroplasticity suggests actual changes take place in the brain.

To recap, when the brain understands that the pain with fibro makes sense to you, it will not react with so much pain when the nerve sensors tell it to respond. So with fibro, the nerve threshold is always ON. The nervous system's fight-or-flight response system turns on one day and stays on. Those with fibro produce more adrenaline and cortisol as a result, which stimulates the nerves and causes more fatigue—constant fatigue. The nervous system forces the pain threshold lower-constant pain.

WHAT TO PRACTICE?

Learn everything you can about fibro until you can explain it to anyone. Talk with your physicians to begin a program that ultimately ends in reducing your pain controlling medications where possible. Begin a regular exercise program. You must increase the blood and oxygen flow around your nerves that are on high alert. Fuel your body with the right diet and you will position yourself for less disease and more wellness. Learn the art of meditation to create a wellness provoking environment. Examine how your work life and your home life (stressors) are impacting your wellness and make a change. Seek cognitive behavioral therapy (CBT) for steps on how to do any of these actions. Consider an anti-depressant medication to help control mood and pain. Stop unhealthy habits and form new healthy habits—starting with diet and exercise. Keep accurate records of your exercise program so you can track your improvements. Make SMART goals. Specific. Measurable. Attainable. Realistic. Timely. Write down what you want from life and what you want from wellness. Then write out what it would take to get there. Then toss out the unrealistic goals and begin going after the other goals. Announce your goals to the world because then you are on the hook and you will begin committing to things again that will boost your self-esteem and confidence. Fill your toolbox with effective coping strategies. Increase your social interaction. Focus on good sleep hygiene. Bedroom is for sleeping and intimacy only. Eliminate all stimulating activities like TV, reading, computer, games, etc., from the bedroom. Do not take naps longer than 20 minutes. Naps are counterproductive to restorative sleep at night. Keep a wellness journal and a gratitude journal. Fire your physician. If you do not have the right clinicians partnering with you, find the right ones.

The future of chronic pain research is broad. Advances need to be made in understanding its etiology, assessment, and treatment. Research is needed in the understanding of how psychological and social factors impact brain processing to determine illness or wellness. The development of newer imaging tools that can look deeper into the brain and nervous system is needed. The study of operant conditioning for chronic pain management may lead to new advances in pain control. Advancing the study of self-management approaches may also lead to better control of pain. It is important to consider the following: What is the relationship between fear and pain? How does catastrophic thinking translate into pain? Does chronic pain produce a cascade of counterproductive behaviors, both cognitive and physiological? Is there a high fear level of addiction and dependence in patient's using opioids?

You can look back in time with many diseases and see that what scientists and physicians thought at one point is not what is believed or proven fact today. With fibromyalgia, like many other illnesses before it, there have been many theories as time passes and are no longer believed to be true. Science is certainly narrowing it down. The goal is less pain, less disability, and improved function and quality of life, and not always a cure.

The treatment methods of chronic illness today are less than sufficient and chronic illness in general continues to pose a large problem for the patient and for society. Adequate pain relief may still be achieved but will likely be done so using complimentary medicine that involves a traditional, psychological, and alternative approach.

We definitely are learning what fibromyalgia is NOT, and we are learning a little bit of what does not work, and that is promising. We are taking this syndrome and shaping it into a disease, one step at a time. Much of what I am proposing is a cumulative collective opinion of many, and much of what I am suggesting is recognized as fact already, and that is extremely promising! We need to continue trying to find the value in chronic illness. Imagine that you have six months to live, which is news that many, many people receive every day. Make a list of everything you did not accomplish in life as a result of illness or whatever the reason. Nothing negative should be on this list. Write down what you CAN still do with chronic illness. Ask yourself what it would take to get from where you are today to where you want to be. I'll tell you what the difference is—it is simply attitude. *You* are standing in the way of living the life you want to live. How do you want to be remembered? Now, go do what you want to do. Leave someone a legacy. Make yourself happy and make someone else proud of the life you are living despite chronic illness. I hope you find some answers in these pages as it has been my goal and pleasure spending years trying to learn as much as I could about unlocking the truth about this misunderstood illness.

REFERENCES

Americans with disabilities act. Retrieved from http://www.ada.gov/

Allsup. Retrieved from http://www.ada.gov/

American Association of Blood Banks. Retrieved from http://www.aabb.org/Pages/Homepage.aspx

American Chronic Pain Association. Retrieved from http://www.theacpa.org/default.aspx

American College of Rheumatology. Retrieved from http://www.rheumatology.org/

American Fibromyalgia Syndrome Association. Retrieved from http://www.afsafund.org/

American Pain Foundation. Retrieved from http://www.painfoundation.org/

American Pain Society. Retrieved from http://www.ampainsoc.org/

Arthritis Foundation. Retrieved from http://www.arthritis.org/

Askmen.com. Retrieved from http://www.askmen.com/

Centers for Disease Control and Prevention. National center for health statistics. Retrieved from http://www.cdc.gov/nchs/

Fibro and Fatigue Centers of America. Retrieved from www.fibroandfatigue.com

Food and Drug Administration. Retrieved from http://www.fda.gov/

Ge, H. (2007). Myofascial trigger points in fibromyalgia syndrome. Retrieved from http://wiki.medpedia.

com/Myofascial_Trigger_Points_in_Fibromyalgia_Syndrome#References

Kubler-Ross, E. (1969). On death and dying. New York, NY.

Mayo Clinic. Retrieved from http://www.mayoclinic.com/

National Center for Complementary and Alternative Medicine. Retrieved from http://nccam.nih.gov/

National Fibromyalgia Association. Retrieved from http://fmaware.org/

National Fibromyalgia Research Association. Retrieved from http://nfra.net/

National Institute of Health. Retrieved from http://nih.gov/

Office of Disability Adjudication and Review. Retrieved from http://ssa.gov/

Stanford University. Retrieved from http://stanford.edu/

APPENDIX A

PHYSICIAN WORKSHEET

Patient Name:_____ DOB:_____Date:_____

Diagnosis:_____

Symptoms:_____

Current list of medications, supplements, vitamins and dosages and schedules: _____

Meds I have used in the past for fibromyalgia or related illnesses: _____

Side effects I have experienced in the past from fibromyalgia treatments: _____

On average I get_____ hours of sleep per night.

My typical diet consists of: _____

My fitness background is:_____

My medical history: _____

Family medical history: _____

My primary care physician is:_____

Other physicians I currently see for other conditions are

_____

Are you an advocate for FM/CFS within reason?

Will your office work with Social Security or disability where applicable?

Are you opposed to written questions and tape recorded visits?

What is your approach to managing my chronic condition?

What is your approach to managing chronic pain alone?

How do you feel about the current fibromyalgia theories that exist today?

Do you recommend cognitive behavioral therapy or a support group?

Does it make sense to treat my condition with a special diet?

What do you recommend to manage my sleep?

What direction should we take to manage my hormone levels?

Do you anticipate that I be treated for infections, fungi or yeasts?

What perpetuating factors do you anticipate my lifestyle, job or other illnesses may be contributing to?

What do my symptoms mean to you?

What is my prognosis? What will my next year entail?

What other physicians do you recommend I pursue?

Are any of my symptoms side effects of medications?

What testing do you recommend going forward and why?

What medications will you prescribe and why? What are the risks?

Where are the best resources for information available?

Can I please have a copy of my records and doctor notes as we progress so that I may manage my care to the best of my ability with my other physicians?

My current abilities or disabilities are:

I used to be able to do the following activities. Now I can do the following activities. I have had to make lifestyle changes to satisfy the limitations of my illness. Currently I use the following assistance in my daily life to get around. The following tasks are no longer a simple consideration for me since my illness has developed: Standing, sitting, walking, climbing, carrying, crawling, pushing, pulling, reaching, grasping, balancing, bending, running, using stairs, jogging, kneeling, squatting, laying, working, keyboarding, reading, writing, meal prep, travel, lifting, shopping, communicating well, talking, phoning, seeing, hearing, smelling, eating, breathing, sleeping, housework, following directions or instructions, comprehending instructions, concentrating, recreational activities, hobbies, going to church, taking meds correctly, making decisions, completing tasks, personal finances, driving, holding objects, being social, visiting others, sexual activity, dressing myself, caring for family, tolerating cold and heat and fumes and noises.

Many of the symptoms below are not categorized as fibromyalgia symptoms and may be unrelated or comorbid.

Symptom list.	Check off.
Muscle pain	IBD-Inflammatory Bowel Disease
Joint pain	MCS-Multiple Chemical Sensitivity
Pain everywhere else	PLMD-Periodic Leg Movement Disorder
Frequent headaches	RLS-Restless Leg Syndrome
Fatigue	Sleep Apnea
Flu-like symptoms	Thyroid disease (typically hypothyroidism)
Extreme sleepiness, insomnia	TMD-Temporomandibular Disease (Jaw Pain)
Sore throats	EBV-Epstein Barr Virus
Difficulty swallowing	HHV6-Human Herpes Virus 6
Frequent choking	Candida Albicans
Feeling bloated/full after eating	Celiac disease
Sensitive hair follicles	CFS-Chronic Fatigue Syndrome
Sensitive skin	Depression
Skin rashes	MVP-Mitral Valve Prolapse
Tumors or lumps	Carpal Tunnel Syndrome
Dizziness	MPS-Myofascial Pain Syndrome
Vertigo/coordination/balance	GERD-Reflux disease
Numbness/tingling	High or low blood pressure
Electrical sensations	High cholesterol or triglycerides
Chest pain, palpitations	Cardiac issues
Heart arrhythmias	Adrenal issues
Memory issues	Hormones issues
Cognition issues (Fibrofog)	Sinusitis or chronic sinus infections
Word recall issues	Extreme thirst

Concentration issues	Drops in blood pressure upon standing
Visual perception issues	Frequent infections
Sensory stimulus issues	Morning sickness, stiffness or hangover
Multi-tasking issues	Anxiety
Painful sexual organs	Panic attacks
Sexual dysfunction	Menstrual issues
Itchy skin	Neuropathic issues
Visual loss	Increase appetite
Blurry/tunnel/spotty vision	Shortness of breath
Loss of libido	Dramatic mood swings
Dry eyes/mouth/skin	Intolerances to stress
Profuse sweating	Stomach pain
Transient paralysis	Nausea
Tremors	Dyslexia issues
Vomiting	Metabolic issues
Alternating diarrhea/constipation	Severe allergies
Low grade fever	Emotional intolerances
Can't regulate climate	Inability to lose weight
Heat or cold intolerances	Bladder issues/ frequent urination
Exercise intolerances	Environmental sensitivities
Delayed fatigue	Extreme junk food cravings

Lab tests: Check off if you have had positive or negative or N/A to help expedite your doctor visit

T3, free	Heavy metal panel
T3 Reverse	Cardio CRP

T4, free

SRT3

T4T3

Thyroid peroxidase

TSH 3rd generation

Estradiol

Progesterone

Testosterone free

Testosterone total

% Free Testosterone

Aldosterone

Fludrocortisone

Cortisol free

Cortisol total

Pregnenolone

Thromboplastin partial time act

ANAchoice

Rheumatoid Factor

Thyroglobulin Anti

Ferritin

Folate, RBC

Vitamin B12

Sex hormone bind glob

Hemoglobin A1c

Epstein-Barr Early AG

EBV IGG VCA by IFA

Chloride

Carbon Dioxide

Blood arsenic

Mercury blood

Lead blood

Homocysteine

DHEA Sulfate

AST

Iron total

Iron binding capacity

Iron % saturation

Nystatin

Magnesium, RBC

Immunoglobulin G1

Immunoglobulin G2

Immunoglobulin G3

Immunoglobulin G4

Immunoglobulin G Serum

Immunoglobulins A

Immunoglobulins G

Immunoglobulins M

Cholesterol total

HDL cholesterol

LDL cholesterol

Triglycerides

Chol/HDLC Ratio

Comp Met Panel w/eGFR glucose

Urea nitrogen (BUN)

Creatinine

eGFR

Calcium

Protein total

Albumin

Globulin

Albumin/Globulin Ratio

Bilirubin total

CBC

Vitamin B6

Insulin

Thrombotic marker panel
D-Dimer, quantitative

Fibrin Monomer

Prothrombin Fragment 1.2

Thrombin-Antithrombin (tat)
Complex

IGF-1

Angiotensin II

TNF Alpha, Highly Sensitive

Cytomegalovirus IGG

Cytomegalovirus IGM

Herpesvirus 6 IGG (HHV-6)

Herpesvirus 6 IGM

Babesia Microti IGG

Babesia Microti IGM

Tissue Transglutaminase
Antibody IGA

Gliadin Antibody IGA (Celiac)

BUN/Creatinine ratio

Sodium

Potassium

Alkaline Phosphatase

Sed rate by modified westergren

ALT

Lipoprotein (a)

Fibrinogen Activity, Clauss

ACTH, Plasma

Natural Killer Cell Functional
Assay, FC

Candida Albicans IGG

Candida Albicans IGA

Candida Albicans IGM

Dihydrotestosterone

Lyme Disease Antibodies

Mycoplasma Pneumoniae IGM

Mycoplasma Pneumoniae IGG

Ehrlichia Chaffeensis IGG

Ehrlichia Chaffeensis IGM

Chlamydophila Pneumoniae IGG

Chlamydophila Pneumoniae IGA

Chlamydophila Pneumoniae IGM

CPK

Aldolase

APPENDIX B

TEN PRINCIPLES TO MANAGING FIBROMYALGIA

1. The first principle is acceptance. You have to accept your illness in full and what has happened to you or you will have trouble moving forward.

2. The second principle is adjusting your attitude. Chronic illness has a way of humbling even the strongest of individuals. Don't stop wanting it all, but stop being defeated when you fail or fall short, because this will cause setbacks. While all of these shortcomings matter, they are also the catalyst for greater disability for many who suffer from an illness. It is our attitude that dictates our coping response-and thus our success at navigating through our illness. Our attitude also helps determine to what extent we will respond to therapy.

3. The third principle is nutrition. With fibromyalgia, your life is complex enough. You need to do everything in your power to increase your chances of successfully beating your illness. By eating right, you eliminate the likelihood of developing nutritional illnesses like type II diabetes, obesity, and general illness associated with poor diet-conditions commonly seen in fibro. While there may not be a cure for fibro today, it is your responsibility to get your body to a condition so that your immune system can do its job of making you well and that starts with diet.

4. The fourth principle is fitness. Without a regular fitness program you will surely become deconditioned and increase your pain and fatigue, and likely other symptoms as well. Exercise helps to control pain levels and tolerance which leads to increased recovery times and proper immune system function-which is one of the ingredients to general wellness. Exercise also releases endorphins-natural pain killers. Join a fitness center because it will commit you to something. It will promote the social aspect of your life that is likely reduced anyway. Make plans to exercise with others because it will put you on the hook to stand by your commitment. Try to go 2-3 times a week. Don't wait to go to the gym until you are not in pain because you will never go. The whole idea is to exercise to reduce symptoms.

5. The fifth principle is stop being the victim. Learn to live again, *with* illness. Stop viewing yourself as someone with limitations and disabilities. Stop catastrophizing.

6. The sixth principle is create a wellness plan. We have reached an era in medicine where the psychological and physical elements of the body are considered one. They are combined, related, and linked in every way imaginable. Wellness, then, is the result of a balance between the physical, emotional, psychological, and the nutritional aspects of humans.

7. The seventh principle is manage your health. You have to manage your condition. Medicine recognizes that the top four aspects of fibro that need to be managed are sleep, hormones, exercise, and nutrition. Stop depending upon clinicians to do it for you. Get back to basics in your life. The earlier you find good clinicians, the better off you will be. Understand your situation. Learn to partner with your doctors. Wellness is your responsibility not your physicians.

8. The eights principle is educate yourself. Education really is key. It is the fundamental ingredient to living a better life. The more you know, the better you will feel. I am certain that through education, I have gained a more complete understanding of my condition which translates into me living better. The lack of knowledge leads to an increase in stress. Get your arms around your condition. Know your disease and you will know what's best for you, you'll know what YOU need to do, and you'll know what your clinicians need to do.

9. The ninth principle is become an advocate. Nothing I have done since I have become chronically ill has been more rewarding, humbling, and attitude adjusting than advocating for fibromyalgia. I have done so in many ways like writing articles for my website, sending hopeful messages to those on Facebook, participating in volunteering like support group meetings, hospice, seminars, and coaching others with fibromyalgia. These actions have enriched my life far beyond the reaches of western medicine. Advocating speaks volumes for your wellness. Get involved, help others like you, and experience the benefits of advocacy. At some point you make the move from helpless victim to advocate in charge of your future. You are in charge of setting the tone for others around you to follow-like family members. As you learn to live with sickness, you slowly realize change.

10. The tenth principle is find hobbies to do. Writing to any degree, participating in social activities, taking advantage of support structure/group. Hobbies take your mind off the pain. Do what you love or find new hobbies that you can do. Having pleasurable activities in your life will add to your quality of life and increase your enrichment. Keep in mind that pacing is the number one thing you can do to

balance out your flares or pain spikes from getting so bad. Get back to positive actions and have fun.

APPENDIX C

BOGUS "CURES"

There are many companies today selling bogus cures for fibromyalgia. I touched on the one I fell for in my most desperate hour who promised to cure me and give me my life back, the Fibro and Fatigue Centers of America. In 14 months of visits to this clinic I sat with dozens of other patients who were anywhere from first visits or going on over two years and I never met anyone who eliminated even one symptom. In fact, most people, myself included had additional symptoms, and while on 75 pills a day which they required that I take, I suffered a stroke. I think desperation is quite a strong motivator when illness has consumed our lives and we have failed to find relief anywhere else. Many of the treatments or cures offered today are sales pitches and are likely to be harmful or cause you a major setback in your recovery.

Companies selling supplements are the worst offenders, focusing on the patients emotions like hope. Miracle cures are a hoax and a scam no matter how reputable they appear. The government does not regulate supplements and most products produced today which allows companies to push their products any way they like. When we suffer from chronic illness, we cannot afford to be the victim so consider the following:

Avoid fast or overnight remedies.

Avoid anything that claims to be a cure.

Avoid strong sales pitches promising to treat many illnesses or disorders.

Avoid sales pitches that use scientific jargon that seems to confuse people.

Avoid companies who put a lot of emphasis on "patient testimonials."

Research the Web about the product you intend to use. If it has lots of complaints or lawsuits, avoid it.

Always discuss what you intend to use with your fibro physician.

Do not buy any health products on the whim. Think about it for a bit before purchasing it.

Research any product you intend to buy on the Web for integrity and quality.

If a celebrity endorses the product, think twice before purchasing it.

APPENDIX D

VALUABLE RESOURCES

Advocates for Fibromyalgia Funding, Treatment, Education, and Research
P.O. Box 768
Libertyville, IL 60048-0766
Phone: 847-362-7807
Fax: 847-680-3922
Email: info@affter.org
Website: http://www.affter.org

Allsup (social security disability representatives)
300 Allsup Place
Belleville, IL, 62223
Toll Free: 800-854-1418
Website: http://www.allsup.com

American Chronic Pain Association
PO Box 850
Rocklin, CA, 95677
Toll Free: 800-533-3231
Email: ACPA@pacbell.net
Website: http://www.theacpa.org

American College of Rheumatology
2200 Lake Boulevard NE
Atlanta, GA 30319
Phone: 404-633-3777
Fax: 404-633-1870
Website: http://www.rheumatology.org

American Pain Foundation
201 North Charles Street, Suite 710
Baltimore, MD 21201
Phone: 888-615-7246
www.painfoundation.org

Arthritis Foundation
P.O. Box 7669
Atlanta, GA 30357-0669
Phone: 404-872-7100
Toll Free: 800-283-7800
Website: http://www.arthritis.org

Centers for Disease Control and Prevention
1600 Clifton Road
Atlanta, GA, 30333
Toll Free: 800-232-4636
TTY: 888-232-6348
Email: cdcinfo@cdc.gov
Website: http://www.cdc.gov

Fibromyalgia Network
P.O. Box 31750
Tucson, AZ 85751-1750
Phone: 520-290-5508
Toll Free: 800-853-2929
Fax: 520-290-5550
Website: http://www.fmnetnews.com

H.O.P.E. Help our Pain & Exhaustion Inc.
Fibromyalgia Awareness, Education, & Support
23915 Forest Park
Novi, MI, 48374
Phone: 248-344-0896
Fax: 248-344-9487
Website: http://www.hffcf.org

National Center for Complementary and Alternative Medicine
P.O. Box 7923
Gaithersburg, MD 20898
Phone: 301-519-3153
Toll Free: 888-644-6226
TTY: 866-464-3615
Fax: 866-464-3616
Email: info@nccam.nih.gov
Website: http://nccam.nih.gov

National Fibromyalgia Association
2121 S. Towne Centre Place, Suite 300
Anaheim, CA 92806
Phone: 714-921-0150
Fax: 714-921-6920
Email: nfa@fmaware.org
Website: http://www.fmaware.org

National Fibromyalgia Partnership, Inc.
P.O. Box 160
Linden, VA 22642–0160
Toll Free: 866–725–4404
TTY: 866–666–2727 (free of charge) or 540–622–2998
Email: mail@fmpartnership.org
Website: http://www.fmpartnership.org

National Institute of Arthritis and Musculoskeletal and Skin Diseases
1 AMS Circle
Bethesda, MD 20892-3675
Phone: 301-495-4484
Toll Free: 877-22-NIAMS (226-4267)
TTY: 301-565-2966
Fax: 301-718-6366

Email: NIAMSinfo@mail.nih.gov
Website: http://www.niams.nih.gov

National Institute of Health
9000 Rockville Pike
Bethesda, MD, 20892
Toll Free: 301-496-4000
TTY: 301-402-9612
Email: NIHinfo@od.nih.gov
Website: http://www.nih.gov

Social Security Administration
Windsor Park Building
6401 Security Blvd.
Baltimore, MD, 21235
Toll Free: 800-772-1213
TTY: 800-325-0778
Website: http://www.ssa.gov